A FAITH ENCOMPASSING
ALL CREATION

The Peaceable Kingdom Series

The Peaceable Kingdom Series is a multivolume series that seeks to challenge the pervasive violence assumed necessary in relation to humans, nonhumans, and the larger environment. By calling on the work of ministers, activists, and scholars, we hope to provide an accessible resource that will help Christians reflect on becoming a more faithful and peaceable people. The series editors are Andy Alexis-Baker and Tripp York.

Volumes include:

VOLUME I: *A Faith Not Worth Fighting For:*
Addressing Commonly Asked Questions about Christian Nonviolence
Edited by Tripp York and Justin Bronson Barringer

VOLUME II: *A Faith Worth Embracing All Creatures:*
Addressing Commonly Asked Questions about Christian Care for Animals
Edited by Tripp York and Andy Alexis-Baker

VOLUME III: *A Faith Encompassing All Creation: Addressing Commonly Asked Questions about Christian Care for the Environment*
Edited by Tripp York and Andy Alexis-Baker

A FAITH ENCOMPASSING ALL CREATION

Addressing Commonly Asked Questions
about Christian Care for the Environment

Edited by
Tripp York
and Andy Alexis-Baker

Foreword by
Bill McKibben

CASCADE *Books* · Eugene, Oregon

A FAITH ENCOMPASSING ALL CREATION
Addressing Commonly Asked Questions about Christian Care for the Environment

The Peaceable Kingdom Series 3

Cascade Books
An Imprint of Wipf and Stock Publishers
199 W. 8th Ave., Suite 3
Eugene, OR 97401

www.wipfandstock.com

ISBN 13: 978–1-62032–650-3

Cataloging-in-Publication data:

A faith encompassing all creation : addressing commonly asked questions about Christian care for the environment / edited by Tripp York and Andy Alexis-Baker ; foreword by Bill McKibben.

xiv + 164 p. ; 23 cm. —Includes bibliographical references.

The Peaceable Kingdom Series 3

ISBN 13: 978–1-62032–650-3

1. Human ecology—Religious aspects—Christianity. I. York, Tripp. II. Alexis-Baker, Andy. III. McKibben, Bill. IV. Title. V. Series.

BT695.5 .F35 2014

Manufactured in the U.S.A.

Contents

Contributors

Andy Alexis-Baker is a PhD candidate in systematic theology and theological ethics at Marquette University. He is coeditor with Theodore J. Koontz of John Howard Yoder's *Christian Attitudes to War, Peace, and Revolution* (2009) as well as coeditor with Gayle Gerber Koontz of Yoder's forthcoming *Theology of Missions* (2013).

Nekeisha Alexis-Baker is an occasional writer and speaker specializing in nonhuman animal ethics and theology, resisting racism, and the intersections of Christianity and anarchist politics. Her recent publications include "The Church as Resistance to Racism and Nation: A Christian, Anarchist Perspective," in *Religious Anarchism: New Perspectives* (2009), and "Doesn't the Bible Say that Humans Are More Important than Animals?" in *A Faith Embracing All Creatures: Addressing Commonly Asked Questions about Christian Care for Animals* (2012). She currently works as a graphic designer for Anabaptist Mennonite Biblical Seminary.

Brenna Cussen Anglada lives at New Hope Catholic Worker farm in LaMotte, Iowa, with her husband and twelve other community members, who are attempting to live the Gospel values of voluntary poverty, hospitality to strangers, and care of creation. Brenna has a master's degree in International Peace Studies from the University of Notre Dame. She has also worked with Michigan Peace Teams, promoting peace in areas of violent conflict such as the West Bank, Gaza, Darfur, and Panama.

Pope Benedict XVI was elected on April 19, 2005, as the 265th pope. Before becoming Pope Benedict XVI, Joseph Ratzinger taught at several universities. He was appointed archbishop of Munich and Freising in 1977, and from 1981 to 2005, he served as the Prefect of the Sacred Congregation for the Doctrine of the Faith. He is author of numerous books, the latest being *A Reason Open to God: On Universities, Education, and Culture* (2013).

Arthur Paul Boers holds the R. J. Bernardo Chair of Leadership at Tyndale Seminary (Toronto). A priest in the Anglican Church of Canada and a Benedictine oblate, he is the author of over half a dozen books, including *The Way Is Made by Walking: A Pilgrimage along the Camino de Santiago* (2007) and *Living into Focus: Choosing What Matters in an Age of Distractions* (2012). Prior to teaching at Tyndale, he taught at Anabaptist Mennonite Biblical Seminary. His website is www.arthurboers.com.

Steven Bouma-Prediger is Professor of Religion and Director of the Environmental Studies Program at Hope College in Holland, Michigan. A graduate of Hope College, his PhD is in religious studies from The University of Chicago. His most recent book is *For the Beauty of the Earth: A Christian Vision for Creation Care*, revised second edition (2010).

Celia Deane-Drummond is Professor of Theology at the University of Notre Dame. She has a doctorate in plant physiology and another in systematic theology. She has authored or edited twenty-two books, including *Creaturely Theology: On God, Humans and Other Animals*, coedited with David Clough (2009); *Seeds of Hope: Facing the Challenge of Climate Justice* (2010); and *Religion and Ecology in the Public Sphere*, coedited with Heinrich Bedford-Strohm (2011).

Samuel Ewell is an ordained Baptist minister and a novice on the way toward Benedictine oblation. In addition to publishing articles and reviews in Portuguese and English, he is also the author of *Building Up the Church: Live Experiments in Faith, Hope, and Love* (2008).

Kelly Johnson is an Associate Professor in the Department of Religious Studies at the University of Dayton. She is the author of *The Fear of Beggars: Stewardship and Poverty in Christian Ethics* (2007) and co-editor of *Unsettling Arguments: A Festschrift on the Occasion of Stanley Hauerwas's 70th Birthday* (2010).

Bill McKibben is the author of a dozen books about the environment, beginning with *The End of Nature* (1989), which is regarded as the first book on climate change intended for a general audience. He is a founder of the grassroots climate campaign 350.org, which has coordinated fifteen thousand rallies in 189 countries since 2009. *Time* called him "the planet's best green journalist," and the *Boston Globe* described him as "probably the country's most important environmentalist." His latest book is *Oil and Honey: The Education of an Unlikely Activist* (2013).

Ched Myers is an activist theologian who has worked in social change movements for thirty-five years. He is a popular educator who animates Scripture and issues of faith-based peace and justice. He has authored over one hundred articles and more than half a dozen books, including *Binding the Strong Man* (1988) and, with Matthew Colwell, *Our God Is Undocumented: Biblical Faith and Immigrant Justice* (2012). His website is www.ChedMyers.org.

Claudio Oliver is a Brazilian urban farmer. He is presently pastoring a multiethnic community of faith in Curitiba, Brazil. In 2011, Claudio and a bunch of scholars and crazy practitioners launched an International Learning Community based on spirituality, organic farming, dialog, and mentoring.

Nancy Sleeth is the author of *Almost Amish: One Woman's Quest for a Slower, Simpler, More Sustainable Life* (2012) and *Go Green, Save Green* (2010), the first-ever practical guide for going green from a faith perspective. Recognized by *Newsweek* and *Christianity Today* as one of the "50 Evangelical Woman to Watch," Nancy is the cofounder of Blessed Earth, a Christian environmental nonprofit.

L. Diane Smith was formerly Assistant Director of Noah's Ark, an animal sanctuary in Locust Grove, Georgia.

William Willimon is an elder in the United Methodist Church. He has served as the dean of Duke Chapel and Professor of Christian Ministry at Duke University for twenty years. From 2004 to 2012, he served as the UMC Bishop of the North Alabama Conference. Willimon is the author of sixty books. His *Worship as Pastoral Care* was selected as one of the ten most useful books for pastors in 1979 by the Academy of Parish Clergy. More than a million copies of his books have been sold.

John Howard Yoder was Professor of Theology at the University of Notre Dame until his death in 1997. He authored many books, including *The Politics of Jesus* (1994). He left behind many unpublished pieces that have since been turned into books, including *The War of the Lamb* (2009) and *Radical Christian Discipleship* (2012).

Laura Yordy is Associate Professor of Philosophy and Religion at Bridgewater College in the Shenandoah Valley of Virginia. She is the author of *Green Witness: Ecology, Ethics, and the Kingdom of God* (2008), as well as several articles and book chapters.

Tripp York teaches in the Religious Studies Department at Virginia Wesleyan College in Norfolk, Virginia. He is the author and editor of numerous books, including *The Devil Wears Nada, Donkeys and Kings,* and *Living on Hope While Living in Babylon.*

Foreword

Bill McKibben

It's been such a pleasure, over the last two decades, to watch the growth of a faith-based environmental movement.

Part of that pleasure is because the effort to save, above all, the climate system needs the moral authority that our religious traditions can provide. It is hard to think of an important nineteenth- or twentieth-century social movement of which the church was not a key part. And already leaders from groups such as Interfaith Power and Light and Interfaith Moral Action on Climate are playing a key role in the expanding fight.

But the bigger part of the pleasure lies in the fact that engagement with this new reality will be challenging and useful to the church—to its theologies, liturgies, and communities. This volume, with its fresh and engaged thinking, makes that point clearly, I think.

Twenty years ago, most liberal churches paid little attention to environmentalism because they assumed it was a luxury item, something you got to once you had taken care of poverty and war. And many more conservative churches, I think, feared it would be a way station on the path to paganism. But reality—the signs of the times, in this case written in the temperature records, the charts of acidifying seawater, the surging tide of extreme weather—has a way of overruling objections, at least for the faithful and the humble.

Over time, then, we have learned that poverty and war are increasingly the handmaidens of environmental destruction. When twenty

million people are forced from their homes in Pakistan by a single season of devastating flood, when a failed harvest on one continent can
drive the cost of food up 40 percent, when cultures thousands of years
old start to sink beneath the waves, it is easier to understand that without a stable planet poverty and war will flourish as never before. I mean,
if the Pentagon now understands it, it is no wonder that the National
Council of Churches has caught on.

And for those who worry about being faithful stewards of God's
creation, our perverse carelessness has gotten so obvious that it takes
an act of will to ignore. Last year we managed to essentially melt the
summer sea ice in the Arctic—that is, we took one of the largest physical features on the planet and broke it. I like Nancy Sleeth's comparison
to trashing a car, but I'd go her one deeper. God asked us to exercise
dominion over this planet, which is not that far from, say, me asking a
babysitter to take care of my daughter for the night. But we're turning
into the babysitter from hell, covering the four-year-old with tattoos
and piercings.

Unlike all the other sins we engage in, this one is new to our time;
it is only in the last few decades that we have had the scientific where-
withal to know what damage we are causing. *And* the scientific where-
withal to know what we should be doing instead: not wasting the sun
and the wind that God washes across our earth every hour of every day,
but putting them to use for the power we need.

Making that transition will require standing up to the most powerful forces on our earth—the richest companies ever seen, grouped
together in the fossil fuel industry. In 2012, Exxon Mobil nearly broke
its own record for profitability, having earned $44.9 billion overall—call
these guys "Powers and Principalities Inc." Confronting them with the
loving firmness that the situation requires will be scary, which is another reason that it is nice our religious leaders are more involved. When
I went to jail on the first day of what turned out to be the largest civil
disobedience action in thirty years in this country—the 2011 campaign
to slow construction of the Keystone Pipeline—it was a great comfort to
see Jim Antal, conference minister and president of the Massachusetts
Conference of the United Church of Christ, three cells down. And it

was a great comfort, too, when Sunday morning dawned behind bars, to sing "Certainly Lord" with the rest of the cellblock.

It is also a great comfort, since we are very far behind in these battles, to be a part of a faith community. We are allowed to hope, I think, that if we do every possible thing we can think of, the world may meet us halfway. We are called to do all that we can. And along the way we are called to witness the beauty of the earth God gave us. It will never be more integral or intact than it is right now—there will never be more crawling creatures or winged birds. Part of our job and our delight is simply to sing that glory. Many thanks to the authors of this fine volume for playing their part in that blessed duty.

Introduction

Andy Alexis-Baker

ON JULY 18, 2003, Carlos Arturo Reyes Méndez, a layperson who worked for the Catholic organization Caritas Honduras, was assassinated. Méndez had helped organize a campaign in which thirty thousand people walked 120 miles to Honduras's capital to protest the clear-cutting of forests in the Olancho region by domestic and international logging companies.[1] Olancho is Honduras's biggest and most biologically diverse area, and it is filled with mountaintop and lowland rain forests as well as old-growth pine forests. Honduran forests as a whole shelter and feed over 232 bird species and 5,680 plant species, many found nowhere else in the world. Moreover, Honduran forests lie at the center of the Mesoamerican Biological Corridor, a conservation passageway stretching from southern Mexico to northern Panama, which allows threatened species such as jaguars and panthers to migrate.[2] Without the corridor, these species would go extinct.[3] Without the Honduran forests, the corridor doesn't serve its intended purpose.

Sadly, unregulated logging has already destroyed half of Olancho's twelve million acres of forest. As a result of the deforestation, local human communities have been deprived of access to water, arable land,

1. Laypersons and priests were participants in this march; even Cardinal Oscar Andrés Rodriguez Maradiaga, archbishop of Tegucigalpa, took part.

2. See White, "Path of the Jaguar."

3. For a critical history of this corridor, including the political quagmires the project has been trapped in, see Fraser, *Rewilding the World*, 62–78.

and their traditional homelands. In addition, Honduras's national bird, the scarlet macaw, is now critically endangered, and several species of parrot, manatees, and big cats are among the numerous nonhuman animals on Honduras's growing endangered list. The country's rich plant life is likewise threatened, with 108 species vulnerable to endangerment. Human communities, too, face great ecological pressures that make surviving off the land increasingly difficult.

Logging companies, in tandem with powerful landowners and crime bosses, control access to the forests. Under their watch, commercial logging has already decimated Honduran mahogany and pine trees. The United States is currently the biggest importer of Honduran timber, the sale of which was declared illegal by national and international treaties. Despite its being a crime to trade in these products, corporations like Home Depot resell the wood to their U.S. clientele, and billionaires like Donald Trump purchase Honduran mahogany for their personal use. Even the U.S. Capitol Building contains items made from Honduran mahogany.[4]

Within Honduras, the primary use of cleared forests is cattle ranching. Yet, the primary reason why Hondurans have developed these new cattle ranches is to export beef to feed people in the United States. From 1960 to 1983, 34 percent of all loans that the World Bank granted to Honduras were for developing new cattle ranches, mainly by clear-cutting the forests.[5] These ranches and their pastures increase soil erosion because tree roots are no longer there to hold the soil in place, further degrading the once fertile land. Moreover, when the forests are gone, the soil is not rich enough to support grazing grasses for more than a few years because rain forests keep the nutrients in the tops of the trees, not in the soil. After a few years, the forest-turned-pasture becomes barren. To make matters worse, because ranches are constructed to have as few employees as possible, they do not provide jobs for the people they displace. Instead, rich landowners profit from exploiting human and nonhuman creation and exacerbate poverty in the nation. Sadly, consumers in the United States and beyond fuel these and other

4. Environmental Investigation Agency, *Illegal Logging Crisis in Honduras*.
5. Stonich and DeWalt, "Political Ecology of Deforestation in Honduras," 293–94.

abuses by purchasing meat and wood products at prices that hide the true ecological, economic, and human costs.[6]

In response to this dire situation, many people in rural Honduras have been diligently opposing the corporate takeover of their land. This resistance comes at great personal risk since local community members who demand an end to the clear-cutting often find themselves in danger and fleeing for their lives. Méndez was one of numerous Catholic environmentalists to have a bounty put on his head. Father José Andrés Tamayo Cortez, founder of Movimiento Ambientalista de Olancho (Environmental Movement of Olancho [MAO]), has also been on death squad hit lists because of his work organizing subsistence farmers and Catholic leaders against commercial logging on their land. In 2003, the mayor of Salamá repeatedly claimed that "the environmental problem in Olancho will only be resolved by ordering the killing of Father Tamayo."[7] To date, Father Tamayo, who has received international awards for his commitment to human rights and environmentalism, has evaded those seeking to kill him.[8] But he was not able to avoid the Honduran government, which stripped him of his citizenship and deported him back to his native El Salvador in 2009.

As a result of the collusion between corporations, the state, the police and military, attacks against Catholic environmentalists in Olancho are ongoing. On December 20, 2006, police murdered two members of Father Tamayo's organization, Heraldo Zúñiga and Roger Murillo. Four police officers were convicted of the murders after pressure from groups such as Amnesty International and Greenpeace forced authorities to take action. On May 8, 2011, masked men ambushed and killed Adalberto Figueroa, yet another Catholic layperson who was part of MAO, as he collected firewood with his eleven-year-old son.[9] Days be-

6. Another by-product of the deforestation is that Hondurans are forced to immigrate because they have few job opportunities in Honduras. The U.S. policy on immigration, which forces many of these Hondurans to enter illegally, is yet another sad aspect of environmental degradation in Honduras.

7. Quoted by Allan Thornton in his introduction to the Environmental Investigation Agency's *Illegal Logging Crisis in Honduras.*

8. See http://www.goldmanprize.org/2005/southcentralamerica.

9. See "Another Environmental Movement Leader Murdered." Online: http://hondurasresists.org/sn_display1.php?row_ID=242&mlang=1.

fore his murder, he had issued a demand to the national forestry service to stop the deforestation and had organized a council to help make the forest a protected area. Because of those efforts, his life was taken.

In chapter 14 of this book, Pope Benedict XVI makes a bold claim: "If you want to cultivate peace, protect creation." Many Catholics in Honduras have taken up that challenge for decades at great cost to themselves and their families. These priests, farmers, bishops, and peasants embody the reason why a book series exploring God's peaceable kingdom must contain a collection of essays on creation care. Far from a marginal issue, the ongoing story in Honduras dramatizes the way in which peacebuilding must take into account protecting nonhuman animals, plants, and the rest of creation. Honduran Catholics and ecologists know that they are part of the rest of creation and that their communities will die off as surely as plant and animal life dies off if the forests come down. It is critical that others around the world—particularly Westerners, who have contributed significantly to the planet's present crisis—understand and embrace this important truth.

About This Book

BEHIND THE VIOLENCE HUMANS perpetrate against each other and against nonhuman creation lies many interconnected beliefs, habits, and traditions. Therefore, when someone calls upon fellow Christians to boycott U.S. department stores that sell products made from illegally harvested wood, to eat less meat from factory farms, or to otherwise reduce the negative impact they have on the earth, she can run into a slew of questions: Isn't creation here simply for our use? Don't we have dominion over all creatures? If we put too much focus on nonhuman creation, won't we begin to worship nature instead of God? Shouldn't we care about human souls above all else? This book offer answers to these and other questions. By taking these questions seriously and answering them without being dismissive, the authors and editors hope to open ourselves to others and to provide witness to an alternative way of living on God's green earth.

But this book is not addressed only to those who are skeptical of the Christian call to peacemaking. Peace-minded Christians who would never take up arms against another human sometimes wear blinders when it comes to nonhuman creatures. One reason for this divide is the fear among peacemakers that caring for creation will take time and energy away from the more immediate task of caring for humans in need. However, the situation in Honduras is a reminder that human-on-human conflicts are not carried out in a vacuum, apart from nonhuman creation. How we treat the land, the water, the air, and other animals has a huge impact on the ways humans treat each other.

The contributors to this volume answer frequently asked questions about creation care: Isn't it more urgent to care for humans than the planet? Isn't it all going to burn anyway? What about Jesus and the fig tree? Each author gives an honest answer while respecting the question. The authors are deeply rooted within the Christian tradition and seek to find and promote the best of the tradition rather than try to reinvent Christian faith from the ground up. Thus, they help us all become more theologically and biblically informed.

Tripp and I have diligently sought a diverse range of contributors. Half of the chapters are written by women. While most of the authors are from the United States, there are also authors from Canada, Great Britain, Brazil, and Germany. Professors, activists, clergy (including the former pope), conservationists, and farmers from a variety of Christian traditions—Catholic, Anglican, Baptist, Methodist, Reformed, African Methodist Episcopal, and Mennonite—are represented in this volume. As we thought about the book, Tripp and I concluded that the diversity of the contributors should in some sense reflect the diversity of God's creation. No book on creation care can do justice to the topic if it is dominated by white American males. We hope that books on Christianity and the environment will become more diverse and that our attempt is a sign of that possibility.

The contributors to this book follow a powerful tradition in Christianity. Genesis 1 repeatedly affirms that nonhuman creation is good. The Psalms are filled with examples of nonhuman creation praising God and of other creatures having intrinsic worth and goodness before God. Throughout the gospels, Christ offers a model of patient servanthood over and against violent subjugation and calls his followers to adopt the same posture. We have included a volume on creation care (and a previous volume on care for nonhuman animals) in the Peaceable Kingdom Series because the biblical vision is that of reconciled relationships, not only between humans but also between humans and creation, and between all of creation and the Creator. As Protestant theologian Karl Barth stated, the human "is first introduced only as the being who had to be created for the sake of the earth and to serve it."[10] The contributors to this book answer the questions their brothers and sisters ask, and they do so in service of creation. We hope it is a service done well.[11]

10. Barth, *Church Dogmatics*, III/1, 235.

11. Thanks to Nekeisha Alexis-Baker and Tripp York for their comments and editing of this introduction. It is much easier to edit other people's work than one's own.

1

What Is Creation For?

Celia Deane-Drummond

IN A POPULAR ARTICLE published in the journal *Science*, historian Lynn White charged that "Christianity bears a huge burden of guilt" for the current ecological crisis.[1] White traces the stark contemporary separation between human beings and their natural environment to Christian accounts of human transcendence over the natural world. Christians, he suggests, not only ignore environmental concerns entirely so they can focus on their souls' salvation, but worse, they have encouraged attitudes of domination that have led to the environmental destruction we see around us. Instead of fostering peace with the natural world, Christian attitudes have wrought environmental destruction by focusing on specifically human needs and wants, treating the environment as a commodity humans can use however we want. He therefore describes Christianity as "the most anthropocentric religion the world has ever seen."[2]

White published his article in 1967. At that time, some people doubted that an ecological crisis existed. Those same people have had to revise their assessment as more and more evidence accumulates

1. White, "Historical Roots of Our Ecologic Crisis," 1203–7.

2. Ibid., 1205. By "anthropocentric," he means focusing on human beings to the exclusion of almost everything else.

documenting the loss of other species, mostly due to habitat destruction, pollution's global and local impacts, indirect and direct impacts of climate change, and the finite limits of natural resources. White's assessment at least prompted some religious leaders and theologians to take creation more seriously. Many objected to his sweeping assessment that Christians were primarily responsible and defended Christian belief, arguing that Genesis 1:28 promotes dominion, not domination, and responsible stewardship, not exploitation.[3] Further, they argued that secularization was the real problem, encouraging a consumerist lifestyle that impacted negatively on the natural world. But might it not be more honest to admit that Christians have been slower than some to acknowledge their part in the problem? Theologians and church leaders may be gradually awakening to this issue, but I suggest that it is *still* not as high on the list of priorities as it deserves to be, given the long-term threat to the *whole of existence*, including the future survival of human beings. Hard evidence continues to accumulate, demonstrating continued losses of threatened, endangered, and extinct species, along with a host of other ecological problems. So half a century after White's diatribe against Christianity, the attention ethicists and theologians have paid to ecology is still less than one might expect, given the scale and scope of the problems involved. So what is to be done?

How Does God Create? Creation through Wisdom

Returning to ancient teachings on creation and its meaning may give us some clues about how to treat the natural world in which we live. The early Genesis stories speak of a Creator God who gives human beings dominion over the natural world. Unfortunately, many Christians interpret *dominion* as mandating *domination* over the nonhuman world, and do so to justify exploitation. But the biblical account of humanity's creation was primarily intended as a prelude to God's saving action toward Israel, recounted in Exodus, rather than a specific account of human or natural origins.

---

3. White's essay also affirmed Eastern Orthodox Christian practices that weave in a more holistic approach to doxology and practice, as well as the example of Saint Francis, who has become ecology's patron saint.

Early Christian theologians tended to interpret Genesis's opening verses as biblical justification for the idea of creation out of nothing (*creatio ex nihilo*), though some contemporary scholars resist such an interpretation.[4] Some scholars also reject creation out of nothing on the basis that it portrays God in a way that gives God too much power over creation. Should we conceive of God differently and think of God as urging creation into existence, perhaps through persuasion rather than out of nothing?[5] I suggest that creation out of nothing, as a theological idea, is still important today, not least because it shows that God affirms all of creation in that it is *God's* creation, while understanding that creation to be finite and distinct from an infinite God.

Does that mean God is remote from and unconcerned with creation, or that God cares for only those creatures most like God, namely, human beings? Certainly not, because God declares creation to be good, created not out of God's need, but out of overflowing love, and *through* wisdom.[6]

But what does goodness mean if there is so much suffering in creation? Does it mean that the Creator's intention is somehow malicious? Again, this is improbable since God repeatedly declares creation to be good. We can ask, however, what creation's goodness might mean. It is unlikely to mean *perfection* in every respect, since clearly there are undesirable aspects of the natural world. It is more likely to mean goodness in relation to God's *intentions*, for God creates in overflowing love.

How do we know that God loves the created world? I suggest that knowing how God acts in human history helps us understand how God creates. This is, after all, the way the Genesis text came to be composed. The love that God shows to a specific people, namely, the Israelites, becomes a metaphor for how God acts in the world at large. Other texts in the wisdom literature also speaks of God's intense love for all of the creation. In Proverbs 8:22, for example, Wisdom is personified as a little

4. Claus Westermann's erudite commentary on Genesis is by far the most comprehensive treatment of the topic to date. Westermann, *Genesis 1–11*.

5. Catherine Keller has argued against creation out of nothing (*creatio ex nihilo*), preferring a process theology view of *creatio ex profundis* instead. See Keller, *Face of the Deep*. For further discussion of this topic, see Deane-Drummond, "Creation."

6. For a more detailed treatment of consideration of the idea of creation in love and through wisdom, see Deane-Drummond, *Creation through Wisdom*.

child, ever at play in creation. Wisdom here is not so much God as God's accomplice in the creative process. Over time, Wisdom came to be identified with the Torah, and in Christian history the Torah with Christ, so the playful purposefulness of Wisdom acting in creation became analogous to the way in which God creates.

What Is Creation's Ultimate Purpose? Celebrating the Sabbath

As we follow the narrative in Genesis 1 and 2, the final day of creation seems to reflect God's good purposes most accurately. When we look at what this purpose might entail we are caught by surprise, for we find that it is a day when God rested and took delight in creation. In resting, God didn't collapse in exhaustion after an intense creative process, suggesting that God found God's own limitations. Nor is the point that God had already completed everything and rested in the satisfied sense that comes from a finished work. Rather, the Sabbath itself culminates God's creative activity, pointing to Sabbath rest as the purpose of creation as a whole. Time is therefore made holy and blessed in the Sabbath.[7]

Jürgen Moltmann has paid close attention to the idea of the Sabbath, pointing out that here we have a finite creation in repose with an infinite God.[8] He suggests that the created world is enabled to flourish in God's presence, rather than being intimidated by God. But he then suggests that created things act on God and that God experiences them somehow. How helpful is it to push these ideas to their limits? Certainly, we can understand such a meaning if it symbolizes the way God is genuinely concerned for and feels compassion for the created world. If this were not the case, then the phrase "God loves creation" would seem shallow and meaningless. But it is important to maintain a clear distinction between God and creation. For if we collapse that distinction and equate God with the natural world, then we have no reconciliation between creatures and God hinted at in the Sabbath; we only have fusion. The point is that in speaking of the relationship between

7. For further discussion of this aspect, see Deane-Drummond, "Living from the Sabbath."

8. Moltmann, *God in Creation*, 278–80.

God and God's creatures there is both distinction and intimacy, a joining in the dance of creation, alongside recognition of God as Lord of all. But how do we really know that God loves the natural world in this way?

One clue comes in the biblical story of Job, who suffers countless trials, purportedly as Satan wanted to prove that Job's love for God was not genuine. As the story goes, eventually Job cracks and wishes that he had never been born, crying out that it would have been preferable for creation to be undone and returned to the chaotic state out of which it began.[9] His accusers attempt to show that Job deserved his suffering. But God, bursting from the whirlwind, proves them wrong. God is Lord of all. All creation exists to celebrate and praise God's name. I suggest that God's speech echoes the Sabbath ideal: God's purpose for the created world is beyond anything that humans can envisage or imagine. So, Job affirms that, like the Sabbath of creation, human beings are not necessarily the crown of creation.

Such a reminder of human frailty in the midst of the world's vagaries, including Leviathan and Behemoth, who in various ways put humanity to shame, should not surprise us. For the story of Job is a way of putting human beings in their place, of resisting the hubris that so often tempts the human species. Humans are creatures like other creatures. In Job, God's providence reaches far wider than simple human interests, for God's care spreads to the world's most remote regions. Job's message is therefore wisdom for today, as it speaks of creation's purpose in praise of the Creator in a particularly clear way. Eventually, God restores Job's fortunes, but suffering has changed Job's perspective. He no longer expects to know God's workings in the created world. He still remains, however, the only creature to whom God directs verbal attention and direct speech, thus indicating a particular responsibility. Hence, the book of Job does not teach a moral lesson about weakening the importance of how human beings act; instead, Job shows the significance of human action in the context of wider concerns. Job's world is

---

9. Bill McKibben also believes that the environmental relevance of Job has been overlooked. McKibben, *Comforting Whirlwind*, xi. I comment further on this aspect in Deane-Drummond, "Creation." For a recent commentary that seeks to draw out the ecological significance of Job, see Schifferdecker, *Out of the Whirlwind*.

an enlarged world, one that is expanded in an inclusive way in relation to other creatures.

Must we be stripped bare like Job before we come to our senses and *only then* appreciate the real value of the natural world? Certainly for Job, at the depth of his despair, God's reply affirmed divine authority over all created things: "Where were you when I laid the earth's foundation? . . . Do you know who fixed its dimensions or who measured it with a line? . . .Who set its cornerstone when the morning stars sang together and all the divine beings shouted for joy?" (Job 38:4–7). But is such a position about God still credible today? Can we really affirm God's authority in the midst of human destructiveness and its impact on the earth? While Job's story ends happily, how do we know if this is really the way God will act?

How Do We Know God Loves the Earth?
Ecology and Deep Incarnation

To understand more fully how God relates to the created world, the New Testament reminds us that such discussion is meaningless without considering the importance and significance of Jesus Christ. A number of scholars have begun to use the language of "deep incarnation" to remind theologians of Christ's wider significance.[10] Just as human responsibility has sometimes been interpreted narrowly in terms of human interests, so Christ's significance has sometimes been restricted to human societies. But the early Christians celebrated Christ for his cosmic and universal significance. The temptation today is to fit Christ into categories that make sense to us, so that weighed down by cultural mores associated with scientific knowledge we tend to restrict the content of our faith accordingly. Christ becomes a diminished Christ, one whom we can more readily believe in for a scientific age. But those scholars who press for deep incarnation want to stress the significance

10. For a pioneering article in this respect, see Gregerson, "Deep Incarnation," 173–87. While Niels Gregerson first coined the term "deep incarnation" to express the evolutionary significance of Christ, Elisabeth Johnson has drawn on this term for its particular resonance in developing a Christology for an ecological era. See Johnson, "Earthly Christology," 27–30.

of Christ not just for humankind, but for all of creaturely kind as well. Biblical warrant for such a move comes from closer reflection on the prologue to John's Gospel, which affirms the Word made flesh.

The miracle of the incarnation concerns the astonishing thought that an eternal God who Christians name as the Creator of the world became embedded in the material world; God becomes a material being. But such a God does not also become disempowered, for God deliberately becomes material, thus demonstrating a love beyond compare. Creation's goodness reaches its zenith at this point in the universe's history. For what greater love is there than this, namely, deliberately forgoing one's powers in order to become like the one we love? The movement of deep incarnation is therefore one from Christ out to the material world. This is not mere idle theological speculation, for biblical witness to such a view comes in Colossians 1, where a celebrated hymn to Wisdom is co-opted to refer to Christ, but now the blood of the cross becomes significant in describing Christ as both through whom all things are created and in whom all things are reconciled. The drama we find in Christ's life becomes all-inclusive, so that all of creation is caught up in that life, death, and resurrection. Creation and its creatures are therefore not simply a stage on which humans act, but part of the activity itself, caught up in reconciliation and ultimately consummation with humanity.[11]

What Does the Reconciliation of All Things in Christ Really Mean?

In answering the question, "What is creation for?" we need to bear in mind what it is *not* for. It is certainly not for our wanton exploitation and rampant misuse. Those collective actions that lead to the natural world's destruction—actions that almost escape our view since they depend on the multiple acts of many individuals—we can name anthropogenic sin, picking up the term *anthropogenic* from climate scientists who want to speak of the specific climatic changes that seem to be related to specifically human actions. In this sense Lynn White is right—

11. For a more detailed account of the arguments for widening theo-drama to include other creatures, see Deane-Drummond, *Christ and Evolution*.

to some extent we are all to blame for the ecological crisis, including Christians. However much we try to live lightly on the earth, we will fall short of what is really required, as we are embedded in social structures and systems that lean towards wasteful practices in their dependence on a market-driven growth economy. Further, those of us who live in the Western world inevitably have a higher carbon footprint than those who live in poorer Southern nations. It would be a mistake to hide and declare innocence when the reality is also *mea culpa*.

Once we begin to recognize the deep significance of the creaturely world—a world affirmed not only by God's presence in creation, but also by a recognition that the incarnation's significance reaches out to all created beings—then the necessity for eco-justice follows. If "environmental justice" is the insight that those who are on the margins of human societies have the right to a clean and healthy environment, then "eco-justice" is about extending justice to other creatures and to those ecosystems in which both humans and other species coexist. Such systems are fragile in that they are open to change, but the extent of their resilience will depend on our responsible actions in accordance with what we know from environmental science. Those species in danger of becoming extinct have no resources to resist the changes confronting them, which makes them very vulnerable. Hence, we humans may need to go further than simply restraining our greedy and exploitative actions. We should also take positive action on behalf of the most vulnerable creatures.

How do we decide which species to save? This is a tricky question, for if we believe that creation as a whole is there to glorify God, then it is not our prerogative to pass judgment on which species need to be saved, based, for example, on pragmatic reasons such as their contribution to global carbon neutrality. Insects, for example, in all their intense variety, may be ignored or even despised by humans, but they are extremely important members of the ecosystems in which all creatures live and thrive. Nonetheless, despite what might be termed "God's extraordinary fondness for beetles,"[12] we are entitled to intelligently discern where best

---

12. A term that has crept into popular use since it was coined by twentieth-century evolutionary biologist J. B. Haldane when asking how we could tell what God was like from God's creation. He knew that beetles were far more numerous than any

to direct our energies. Vulnerable human societies and their ecological needs also must be considered alongside other vulnerable creatures. It would go too far to suggest that other animals need to be given preference, as some radical environmental ethics advocates have indicated.[13]

How Should We Live? Living Lightly on the Earth

The affirmation of all life, then, is integral to Christian faith, even if we have tended to push this into the background. One of the great Franciscan medieval theologians, St. Bonaventure, recognized the value of the natural world and affirmed the study of natural sciences in helping us see what he termed the "vestiges of the Trinity." Bonaventure didn't mean that such study would persuade us to acknowledge God; rather, he meant that natural revelation was perceptible through the eyes of faith. He imagined a ladder on the way to God, which begins by recognizing God in all things, and his mystical approach acknowledges that we do not understand everything about the natural world, reminding us of the mystery that is God. It is, though, the luminosity of faith that allows us to see God reflected in the world, but once seen, the life of God in the life of the world becomes crystal clear. "Whoever, therefore, is not enlightened by such splendor of created things is blind; whoever is not awakened by such outcries is deaf; whoever does not praise God because of all these effects is dumb; whoever does not discover the First Principle from such clear signs is a fool," Bonaventure writes.[14] Above all, Bonaventure wants readers to apply their heart so that in creatures the praise of God may become heard and visible once more. By implication, we learn to live lightly on the earth and to treat the creaturely world as in kinship with human beings, rather than in competition with us.

Is a Franciscan approach overidealized? Certainly, Bonaventure did not directly address other creatures in the manner clear in Francis of Assisi's poem "Canticle of Brother Sun." He also construed humanity

---

other species; at the time of his writing there were three hundred thousand species of beetles known, compared with nine thousand bird species and ten thousand mammal species. Today the figure for beetle species is closer to four hundred thousand.

13. See, for example, Rolston, "Feeding People versus Saving Nature?"

14. Bonaventure, "Soul's Journey into God," 67.

as acting like a gardener on the earth, so that while some interaction was necessary, it was done with a specific good purpose in mind.

What about "Natural" Suffering?

A final objection to the idea that God cares for creation or that it is good comes from reflection on the extent and pervasiveness of creaturely suffering in ecological systems. Even that great naturalist Charles Darwin was disturbed by the apparent cruelty in the way in which different species preyed on each other. In exploiting other creatures, are we not simply being like them and following our instincts? Yet, if we look closely at patterns of predation and prey, it is very rare to find creatures taking far more than they need for their own survival. Suffering among nonhuman animals presents us with a problem of how to believe in a good God, but suffering does not mean those creatures are outside God's care. Instead, deep incarnation can encourage us to view creaturely suffering in solidarity with Christ's suffering. Our image of God is therefore too small if we limit it to the human sphere of suffering. The purpose of nonhuman animal suffering can be rationalized through ecosystems and evolutionary theory, but it still confronts us with a deeper mystery of why it needs to be this way. Accounts that stress the relative agency of other creatures in analogy with human freedom are not all that convincing.

I suggest we will never know the full answer to the question of suffering among nonhuman creatures, any more than we will know the full answer to the tragedies that we encounter in our own personal lives. We are confronted with a choice of faith: do we choose to believe in a God who will ultimately make all things new or not? Christian faith insists on the former, grounded in the hope we have in the resurrection of Christ, who entered into the material world in its depth of suffering but whose body was made new again, a body transformed but still recognizable and bearing the marks of his sojourn on earth. The hoped-for new heaven and new earth should, therefore, be the horizon in which we think and consider how to treat the nonhuman world. But it is not a horizon that beckons us to distance ourselves from the creaturely world in which we are embedded, since that new earth is a renewed earth, bearing the footprint of our actions and reactions, just as Christ's body still bore the wounds in his hands, feet, and side. It is, therefore, in the light of eternity, properly conceived, that we gain a clear insight into how to treat the earth here and now—living lightly and appreciating the earth in all its glorious wonder as the work of God the Creator and redeemer. It is in this spirit that we will develop the wisdom to act aright, so that we will know more clearly what creation might be for in our own lives and learn to love that creation as God loves, spurred on by hope and nurtured by faith in a God who is deeply incarnate.

2

Doesn't Creation Care Confuse Nature with God?

Steven Bouma-Prediger

"You must be a tree-hugger," exclaimed a listener after hearing a lecture on creation care that I gave at a Christian liberal arts college a few years ago. "And tree-huggers," he continued, "confuse nature with God. They worship creation instead of the Creator. Orthodox Christians don't confuse nature with God."[1] A hush came over the audience, perhaps due to the direct (and somewhat adversarial) nature of this person's assessment. I knew from previous talks on similar campuses that others in the audience probably had similar concerns. They, too, were wondering how I would respond.

I readily admitted that I was a "tree-hugger," if by that one meant a tree-lover. White pine and red maple, baby balsam fir and ancient giant sequoia, American beech and Canadian hemlock—I love them all. But I vigorously disputed the spurious charge that tree-huggers confuse nature with God. Perhaps some "tree-huggers"—people who care for the earth and its plethora of creatures—do confuse nature with God, but many do not. And Christian earth-keepers, if they know the basic

---

1. Terms such as *nature, creation, world*, and *earth* are not synonymous and need clarification. But for this essay I will use them as more or less equivalent to the biosphere of our home planet. For more on this, see Bouma-Prediger, *For the Beauty of the Earth*, xiv–xv.

beliefs of their faith, do not confuse the two. Indeed, I said to my questioner, it is precisely because I worship God the Creator that I try to care for trees and other creatures God has made.

What usually lies behind the question "Doesn't creation care confuse nature with God?" is the concern that people worship the earth rather than the Creator of heaven and earth. This is a legitimate concern about worshipping the wrong thing. To worship creation rather than Creator is idolatry. So underneath this question is a concern worth respecting. But that only raises the question, is it true that Christians who care for creation confuse nature with God?

In response, I will make three basic points. First, creation care does not necessarily presuppose nature worship. It simply does not follow that caring for the earth and its creatures implies worshipping the natural world. Second, the Christian doctrine of creation, rightly understood, describes a God both different from and intimately involved in the world God creates and sustains and will one day bring to perfection. Third, the call to care for creation is found throughout Scripture and church history. Creation care is anything but heterodox. It is, rather, a fitting response of gratitude to the loving God who made and sustains this world of wonders.

Nature Is Not God, but It Is God's

The first point is simple and short, but important: care for creation does not necessarily presuppose nature worship. In other words, it does not logically follow that caring for the earth and its creatures implies we must worship the natural world. To assume that creation care confuses nature with God is a logical fallacy called a *non sequitur*, which in Latin means "it does not follow." It does not necessarily follow because one can care for something without worshipping it.

As any parent knows, you need not worship your children to care for them. Indeed, we care about lots of things without feeling that they are worthy of worship. My wife, Celaine, loves and cares for our dog, Rosie, though she does not worship her or think her divine. I love and care for the trees I planted for each of my three daughters, even though I do not worship them. My friend Kent loves and cares for the

Adirondacks, even though he does not think that the six-million-acre preserve in upstate New York is a part of God. So we can love and care for people, animals, plants, and even entire ecosystems without divinizing or worshiping them.

The question "Doesn't creation care confuse nature with God?" implies that caring for creation necessarily requires blurring the distinction between Creator and creation, turning the earth into something divine or worthy of worship. The question seems to wrongly presuppose that all who speak of creation care, earth-keeping, or environmental stewardship must believe that nature is Nature—a semidivine or godlike entity that we must reverence. Said differently, while some people might care for the natural world because they see it as divine or godlike, such a worldview is not a requirement for care. Respect does not require reverence. Care does not require veneration. In order to care, I must believe something is valuable, but I need *not* believe it to be divine or worthy of worship. We can explain or defend our care for the earth without viewing nature as divine.

Behind this discussion is an important distinction between classic Christian theism and both deism and pantheism.[2] In deism (*deus* is God in Latin), God exists and creates, but then God goes on holiday. The world runs quite nicely without God. God does not actively sustain the world. Pantheism states that everything is God—*pan* (all) + *theos* (God) in Greek. Creation and God are one and the same. There is no distinction between God and the world. As I will detail further in the next section, the mainstream Christian tradition espouses neither deism nor pantheism. The established Christian tradition does not take creation to be divine, but it does vigorously affirm that creation is sacred or holy. American author Wendell Berry captures this affirmation with particular insight and clarity: "We are holy creatures living with other holy creatures in a world that is holy."[3]

So the world is holy or sacred, but not divine or godlike. British New Testament scholar Richard Bauckham makes this point especially well: "Many Christians have been suspicious of green attitudes to the

2. There are other options, such as panentheism, which some Christians advocate. For more on this, see Bouma-Prediger, *Greening of Theology*, especially chs. 4 and 7.

3. Berry, *Sex, Economy, Freedom, and Community*, 99.

world because they fear some sort of pantheism. The Bible, they point out, has de-divinized the creation. True, but I would say it has not de-sacralized creation. As creatures who belong to God their creator, the non-human creatures are not divine, but they are sacred to God."[4] In other words, the world is not God, but is set apart for service to God. Thus Bauckham argues we must recognize that "the alternative to a spirituality that despises the created world does not have to be one that divinizes the created world. . . . It can be one in which the created world is sacred and valued for love of its Creator who always surpasses it. Love of the Creator can include the creation without being reduced to love of the creation."[5] The Christian alternative to the prevalent contemporary attitude of seeing the natural world as devoid of intrinsic value and valuable only as a means to an end is not to deify the world but to acknowledge that the world is sacred. If the natural world is sacred, then it has value not primarily (or only) because of the commodities it provides, but fundamentally because it is a work of the creating, sustaining, and redeeming God.

In sum, for the Christian tradition the natural world is not divine but sacred. As the pioneering twentieth-century theologian Joseph Sittler succinctly put it, "The world is not God, but it is God's."[6] Hence, Sittler continues, "God is not identified with the world, for He *made* it; but God is not separate from this world, either, for *He* made it."[7] Therefore, Christian creation care does not confuse nature with God or imply the worship of nature. Let's dig a bit deeper into these affirmations.

What Christians Believe about Creator and Creation: A Love Story

What do Christians believe about Creator and creation, about God and the earth? The classic Christian view can be summarized in terms of what I call "The Seven *D*s."[8] My former teacher, Bernard McGinn, pres-

4. Bauckham, *Living with Other Creatures*, 222.

5. Ibid., 209.

6. Sittler, "Ecological Commitment as Theological Responsibility," 178.

7. Sittler, *Structure of Christian Ethics*, 4.

8. Bouma-Prediger, "Creation as the Home of God."

ents "four basic constituents of the idea of creation" found in Christian theology in what he calls "The Four *Ds*": *distinction, dependence, decision*, and *duration*.[9] I enlarge McGinn's list to include three more ingredients: *design, defect*, and *delight*. For each theme I describe several affirmations concerning both creation and God.

Distinction. Central to Christian belief is a fundamental ontological distinction. God is different from what is not-God. For example, creation is finite while God is infinite. Creation is created while God is uncreated. These statements clarify what is meant by speaking of God as transcendent. God's transcendence does not mean God is distant; it means, rather, that God is different from us and all other creatures. As indicated in the previous section, creation is not divine or quasi-divine and God is not the same as or part of creation.

Dependence. Equally central to the Christian tradition is the conviction that creation depends on God for its very existence. Creation is contingent while God is self-existent.[10] Without God's sustaining Spirit, declares Psalm 104, nothing could or would exist. As creator and sustainer, God is immanent in, with, and under creation. These affirmations rule out another set of alternative viewpoints, such as an ontological dualism in which matter is seen as ultimate with or independent of God. Creation is not self-originating, self-perpetuating, or self-explanatory. So deism is denied. God is not aloof or on holiday. The world is not a machine that runs on its own. While creation is not God, it is God's. That is, God brings creation into existence out of love and infuses it with God's own animating and sustaining breath.[11] Creation depends on the God who is love.

Decision. Christians also confess that God did not have to create. The doctrine of creation out of nothing (*creatio ex nihilo*) implies this. Creation is both ontologically and existentially contingent. That means that God did not have to create any world at all, and nothing

9. McGinn, "Do Christian Platonists Really Believe in Creation?" 208–9. McGinn states that the list is not exhaustive, but rather "a heuristic device for raising some of the right questions" concerning the adequacy of a given doctrine of creation.

10. Morris, *Our Idea of God*, 157.

11. The image is from Calvin, *Institutes*, 1.13.14. Calvin there says, "It is the Holy Spirit who, everywhere diffused, sustains all things, causes them to grow, and quickens them in heaven and earth."

obligates or forces God to create this particular world. Creation need not be. It is, rather, a gracious act of a loving God. Indeed, the most central claim Christians make is that God is love. These affirmations call into question certain historically prevalent perspectives. For example, both a Platonic origins story, in which the creator is externally limited by recalcitrant matter, and a Neoplatonic story of origins, in which a principle of plenitude (or overflowing fullness) necessitates that God create, are incompatible with the standard Christian view of God's loving power and powerful love.[12] Creation could not have been. It exists only because of God's love.

Duration. Following the great sixth-century theologian Boethuis and the mainstream Christian tradition, the fourth theme affirms that creation is temporal, whereas God is eternal. Creation comes to be in or with time. God the Creator, in contrast, stands outside of time altogether. These affirmations deny that creation is eternal and that God is temporal. Even those who argue that God is best viewed as everlasting (and thus temporal in some respect) rather than eternal still insist that, however God is in time, God is temporal in a quite different way than creatures.[13] While able to act in time, God is also the maker and master of time. God's relationship to time is unique—unlike that of any creature.

Design. Another central Christian conviction is that creation is both orderly and purposive. Creation is a cosmos—a universe of patterned regularity—and hence intelligible. Creation is, furthermore, an intentionally ordered cosmos. It exhibits the order it does for a reason, namely, because the loving Creator made it so. As Psalm 104 declares, creation is fashioned in wisdom to manifest the glory of a creating and sustaining God. These affirmations imply that chaos does not ultimately define the world. The world's order is not entirely arbitrary or random. Also rejected is any view that construes God as nonpersonal or capricious. God is neither like Aristotle's unmoved mover—thought endlessly thinking its own thoughts—nor like so many of the impulsive and fickle Greek gods. Creation exhibits the order it does because a wise and loving God made it that way.

12. Morris, *Our Idea of God*, 148–49.
13. Wolterstorff, "God Everlasting."

Defect. For Christians, creation is essentially good. So, for example, finitude is good. Being a creature is good. Evil is a perversion of God's intentions for creation—an accidental quality rather than an essential property. The fall, in other words, is contingent, not necessary. God is, by contrast, necessarily good—an implication of God's steadfast love. These affirmations are intended to refute a variety of commonly held beliefs, for example, that finitude is evil or that evil is woven into the warp and weft of creation. Contra Gnosticism or Manicheanism (historical names for the two previous examples), Christians do not believe evil is intrinsic to creation.

Delight. An often overlooked aspect of the Christian doctrine of creation is the conviction that creation, in all of its indescribable variety, is a place of beauty and enjoyment and is of value simply because God made it. In the effusiveness of divine grace, God has created and continues to sustain a plethora of creatures whose existence provokes wonder and whose value extends beyond their usefulness to humans. Instrumental value to humans is only one of many values nonhuman creatures have. So God is not only a faithful supplier of things needful, but also a generous giver of that which evokes joy. These claims challenge the powerful worldview of anthropocentric utilitarianism that finds creation valuable only insofar as it serves human needs and wants. In contrast, according to the biblical Christian tradition, creation is valuable irrespective of its usefulness for humans. And God is not miserly or stingy; rather, God is generous beyond imagining in creating a world both bountiful and beautiful.

In sum, these "Seven *D*s" attempt to describe in technical theological language the love story that Scripture narrates between God and the world. The Christian doctrine of creation describes a God of powerful love, both different from and intimately involved in the world, who creates and sustains the universe and will one day bring it to completion and perfection.

Faithful Ecological Discipleship: Creation Care and the Christian Tradition

So if it does not follow that caring for the earth and its creatures implies worshipping the natural world, and if the Christian doctrine of creation describes a God both different from and intimately involved in the world, then it is a serious mistake to think that Christian creation care confuses nature with God. Creation care by Christians, on the contrary, expresses faithful ecological discipleship—a way of saying thank you to God by caring for what God has created, is sustaining, and will one day completely redeem.

In recent years many authors have written about the Bible and creation care, so I will not attempt to do so here.[14] Suffice it to say, from Genesis to Revelation the Bible presents a powerful vision of God as the loving Creator, Sustainer, and Redeemer of a creation crafted to sing praise to God, including we human earth creatures who bear God's image by serving and protecting the earth.

But what of the Christian tradition? Lest you think this biblical vision has been lost, listen to these voices from the great long story that is the history of the church:

> O God, enlarge within us the sense of fellowship with all
> living things: our brothers and sisters the animals to whom
> in common with us you have given this earth as home. We
> remember with shame that in the past we have exercised
> the high dominion of man with ruthless cruelty so that the
> voice of the earth, which should have risen to you in song,
> has turned into a groan of travail. May we realize that all
> these creatures also live for themselves and for you, not for
> us alone. They too have the goodness of life as we do, and
> serve you better in their way, than we do in ours.
>
> —Basil of Caesarea, late fourth century[15]

---

14. See, for example, Bauckham, *The Bible and Ecology*; Brown, *The Seven Pillars of Creation*; Davis, *Scripture, Culture and Agriculture*.

15. Quoted in Scully, *Dominion*, 13.

Then there is the beauty and utility of the natural creation, which the divine generosity has bestowed on man. . . . How could any description do justice to all these blessings? The manifold diversity of beauty in sky and earth and sea; the abundance of light, and its miraculous loveliness, in sun and moon and stars; the dark shades of woods, the color and fragrance of flowers; the multitudinous varieties of birds, with their songs and bright plumage; the countless different species of living creatures of all shapes and sizes, among whom it is the smallest in bulk that moves our greatest wonder—for we are more astonished at the activities of the tiny ants and bees than at the immense bulk of whales. Then there is the mighty spectacle of the sea itself, putting on its changing colors like different garments, now green, with all the many varied shades, now purple, now blue.

—Augustine, early fifth century[16]

God is above all things by the excellence of his nature; nevertheless He is in all things as causing the being of all things.

—Thomas Aquinas, mid-thirteenth century[17]

Meanwhile let us not be ashamed to take pious delight in the works of God open and manifest in this most beautiful theater [creation]. . . . From this history [in Gen 1–2] we shall learn that God by the power of his Word and Spirit created heaven and earth out of nothing; that thereupon he brought forth living beings and inanimate things of every kind, that in a wonderful series he distinguished an innumerable variety of things, that he endowed each kind with its own nature, assigned functions, appointed places and stations; and that, although all were subject to corruption, he nevertheless provided for the preservation

16. Augustine, *City of God*, 22.24 (Bettenson, 1075).
17. Aquinas, *Summa Theologiae*, 1.8.1.

of each species until the Last Day. We shall likewise learn that he nourishes some in secret ways, and, as it were, from time to time instills new vigor into them; on others he has conferred the power of propagating, lest by their death the entire species perish; that he has so wonderfully adorned heaven and earth with as unlimited abundance, variety, and beauty of all things as could possibly be, quite like a spacious and splendid house, provided and filled with the most exquisite and at the same time most abundant furnishings.

—John Calvin, mid-sixteenth century[18]

When we turn the attention of the church to a definition of the Christian relationship with the natural world, we are not stepping away from grave and proper theological ideas; we are stepping right into the middle of them. There is a deeply rooted, genuinely Christian motivation for attention to God's creation, despite the fact that many church people consider ecology to be a secular concern. "What does environmental preservation have to do with Jesus Christ and his church?" they ask. They could not be more shallow or more wrong.

—Joseph Sittler, late twentieth century[19]

This short sampling of quotations makes clear at least two things. First, from these mainstream thinkers within the Christian tradition there is little danger of confusing nature with God. We should care for creation precisely because God is, as the Apostles' Creed puts it, "the maker of heaven and earth." Second, while some Christians have depreciated the earth and sanctioned its misuse, a long tradition of earth-keeping exists within the church.[20]

Doesn't creation care confuse nature with God? While some tree-huggers may confuse nature with God, I hope by now it is clear that

18. Calvin, *Institutes*, 1.14.20.

19. Sittler, *Gravity and Grace*, 15.

20. On the ecological riches of the Christian tradition, see, for example, the trilogy of Santmire: *The Travail of Nature*, *Nature Reborn*, and *Ritualizing Nature*.

Christian earth-keepers need not (and should not) confuse the world God made with the God who makes and sustains it. We can love the Creator without worshipping creation. May God bless our efforts at faithful ecological discipleship, for they represent our grateful responses to God's gracious gifts and are concrete ways we show our care for the earth.

3

Isn't It More Urgent to Care for Humans than the Planet?

Brenna Cussen Anglada

Someone will say: you worry about birds: why not worry about people? I worry about both birds and people. We are in the world and part of it, and we are destroying everything because we are destroying ourselves, spiritually, morally, and in every way. It is all part of the same sickness.

—Thomas Merton[1]

I RECENTLY HAD THE opportunity to ask a cloistered Trappistine Sister, who had just celebrated sixty years of cloistered, monastic life, about the current lack of vocations to religious orders. She told me that people today don't have the same sense of God in all things that they did even two generations ago. "Even if they're religious, they're too focused on money, or the latest technology. Why would they want to give their lives to a God they only see in church on Sunday?"

Just before Sister Regina entered the monastery, she had read a book by Bishop Fulton Sheen titled *The Life of All Living*. She told me that as soon as she had read that title, "I thought, 'This is it. This is true.'

1. Merton, *Turning Toward the World*, 274.

And I wanted to give my entire life, my entire self, to this God, Who is life itself." If the church is going to see more vocations, she mused, it will need to find a way to reteach and to reinfuse this sense of awe and reverence for all of God's creation, so that people will be able to more fully comprehend the reality of their direct contact with God in all of creation and in every moment.

Sister Regina's response touched the core of what I see as a fundamentally flawed assumption from which many in society, the political sphere, and our churches make decisions and act: that God created the world for human use, but humanity is ultimately separate from the created world and can reach its fullest potential independently of it. Such a misunderstanding has encouraged a pattern of endless human consumption, wreaking havoc not only on the environment but also on human health. People are dependent on the created world, not only in order to survive physically, but also in order to cultivate an awareness of the presence of God and to flourish spiritually.

The opposite, though equally flawed, worldview—a worldview I believe has grown as a direct and extreme response to the ideas above and that is held by a widening segment of environmentalists—is that the earth would do better without humans altogether, and that nature should be left alone in its "perfect" state. Such a position has drawn sharp criticism and accusations from prominent Christians such as former presidential candidate and Catholic believer Rick Santorum, who accused people who care about creation of prioritizing "care for the planet" over "care for people." Unfortunately, such critiques are sometimes accurate. Among environmental and political activists, many of those who humbly recognize the breath of God in an old Sequoia, for example, and who will sacrifice time, comfort, and relationships in order to prevent its destruction, do not also recognize God's own image in the life of an unborn person. Or some who courageously defend the dignity of nonhuman animals by opposing the practices of factory farms and by supporting the local organic food movement, or by adopting a vegan lifestyle, are not equally outraged by the warehousing of elderly or impaired persons in nursing homes where, at best, their physical, emotional, and spiritual health atrophies, and at worst, they are subjected to "mercy killings."

Must there be such a sharp dichotomy between those who prioritize "people over the planet" and those who prioritize "the planet over people"? Those who emphasize the sanctity of human life plead with us to be vigilant, not to let the political trends of the day deceive us into believing that some human lives are expendable in the overall struggle for freedom, justice, and choice. On the other hand, those who emphasize care for the environment are calling us back to a right relationship with God's creation, a relationship of reciprocity and limits that existed in Eden, instead of the current, one-sided relationship of greed. Both voices speak part of the truth, but neither can be truly prophetic unless each recognizes the validity of the other.

Saint Paul, in his letter to the Romans, says that creation itself "awaits with eager expectation the revelation of the children of God" and will "share in the glorious freedom of the children of God" (Rom 8:21). If the salvation of creation is bound up with human salvation, as Paul says, then so is human salvation bound up with creation, which offers us an authentic connection to the divine. The life of a Christian, then, must witness to this holistic ethic and reflect the awareness of the interdependence of human life and the created world.

Christianity has a long tradition of cultivating reverence for creation and the sacredness of the material world. In the very first chapter of Genesis, we are told repeatedly that God created the world and all things in it, and that God saw that those were good. This theme is echoed throughout Scripture. In the book of Daniel, God's servants sing of all earthly creatures, animate and inanimate, as giving glory to God (Dan 3:57–88). In the Gospels, Jesus reminds us of God's love for the wildflowers and the birds of the air (Matt 6) and even encourages us to emulate the relationship that these created beings have with God.[2]

As a Catholic Christian I am deeply inspired by the church's strong emphasis on the realities of the Incarnation (God becoming flesh) and the resurrection of the body, which have served as a balance to the gnostic and modern tendencies to denigrate the physical world. The Catholic tradition takes the sanctity of matter very seriously in its central sacrament of the Eucharist, for example, which depends on the physical pres-

2. See N. Alexis-Baker, "Doesn't the Bible Say that Humans Are More Important than Animals?" 43–46.

ence of bread, "fruit of the earth," and wine, "fruit of the vine," in order to take place. Even the doctrine of the Assumption, though controversial among Christians (because it seems to divinize Mary), is understood by Catholic theologians to further emphasize the dignity and holiness of the physical: "[It] is of supreme importance not only to Catholics, but to all men and women, because it means that there is still in the world, there will always be in the world, a voice to affirm and a power to defend the dignity and ultimate glory of matter, of material things."[3] And many of our beloved saints—among them Hildegard of Bingen (1098–1179 CE), Thomas Aquinas (1225–1274 CE) and, of course, Francis of Assisi (1181–1226 CE)—hold a deep reverence for the created world.

More recently, the Trappist monk Thomas Merton (one of Sister Regina's inspirations) humbly delighted in God's creation so much that he lived the final years of his life in the woods around the Abbey of Gethsemani in rural Kentucky, surrounded by the rhythms of nature, which he believed returned him to a "direct and humble contact with God's world [and] His creation."[4] Merton, in part through his encounters with nature, as well as through his reading in ecology, came to believe that cities—as opposed to God's natural creation—contributed to people's malaise because they were filled with noise and technology, stink and sterility, glitter and trash. "Everything in modern city life is calculated to keep man [*sic*] from entering into himself and thinking about spiritual things," Merton wrote in *No Man Is an Island*.[5] Though Merton was a sharp social critic, he was primarily distressed by the disconnection between people, their ecological context, and their ability to live spiritual lives. Once these connections could be restored, he held, a true culture of peace could take root. Merton thought it vital for monks and others to dwell in the country and wilderness as a way to protect it from society's encroachment and destruction. To remain spiritually alive, people must have contact, in one way or another, with the beauty of creation.

Many of Merton's ecological concerns have been echoed in the witness of the Catholic Worker movement (a movement to which I

3. Vann, *Water and the Fire*, 175–76.

4. Merton, *Dancing in the Water of Life*, 223.

5. Merton, *No Man Is an Island*, 108–9.

belong). Beginning in the 1930s, Peter Maurin, the intellectual cata-
lyst behind the Catholic Worker movement, sought to create a society
"where it is easier to be good" and believed, like Merton, that this was
much easier through a closer connection with the earth. Peter saw the
evils of industrialism rampant in the cities, which he believed were a
profound obstacle to creating a whole and spiritual life. It was impossible for any culture to be healthy, Maurin said, "without a proper regard
for the soil," and his solution to the ills of society lay in the creation of
farming communities that would grow what they ate, perform manual
labor, take time to rest and rejoice in the beauty of the natural world,
and live together communally.[6]

But Peter did not advocate that those privileged enough to purchase land and live a simpler way of life should abandon the poor who
live in the cities. His program for reconstructing society consisted of
three parts: the establishment of farming communes, setting up houses
of hospitality in impoverished urban neighborhoods to serve the poor,
and hosting roundtable discussions to clarify thought around important
political, philosophical, and theological issues of the day (Peter agreed
with Lenin that we can't have a revolution without a *theory* of revolution[7]). Peter's ultimate vision for a thriving, vibrant society, however,
did culminate in a return to communities based on the land, dependent
on the land, and respectful of the land.

A French emigré, Peter grew up at the end of the nineteenth
century in a peasant family living in a rural, Catholic village. He was
deeply informed by the then-emerging French philosophy of personal-
ism, which holds that, as the human person is made up of body, mind,
and spirit, then in order for a culture to flourish, every institution and
organization in that culture should be ordered to cultivate the physical,
mental, and spiritual aspects of the person. Peter saw farming communities to be an ideal setting to develop all three: a person could use her
body to perform satisfying manual labor, explore her creativity in order
to fashion useful, beautiful crafts, and feed her spirits with an experience of the Divine in creation. The farmer's life, too, Peter believed, lent

6. Maurin, *Easy Essays*, 101.

7. Ibid., 15.

itself to more time for study and prayer, fostering an integrated balance between physical, mental, and spiritual work.

At New Hope Catholic Worker Farm outside Dubuque, Iowa, our four-family community is experimenting with Peter's program for reconstructing society by attempting to balance manual work (intensive gardening, animal husbandry, heating and cooking with wood, etc.), spiritual work (daily meditation on the Gospels and silent prayer), and intellectual work (via frequent discussions, study, and workshops on important issues of the day such as technology or the economy). We also offer hospitality on a small scale to travelers and wayfarers, as well as to the occasional person in need of shelter due to lack of money, sobriety, or both. The opening paragraph of our community's covenant sums up our attempt to live a holistic Christian witness, honoring both humanity and the created world: "As a Catholic Worker farm community rooted in the vision of our founders Peter Maurin and Dorothy Day, and guided by our faith in a loving God, we seek to transform ourselves and society by living lives filled with joy, a joy that ripples to every person we encounter and into the world. We seek to steward, celebrate, and share the abundance of God's creation in such a way that we as a community, and all on earth, might flourish together in justice and peace."

We at New Hope are grateful to be only one experiment, one small manifestation of a larger movement that is seeking to create a way forward through an integrated approach of care for the earth and care for people. More broadly, Catholic Worker Houses of Hospitality offer shelter, meals, showers, health care, support, and loving relationships to the poor while growing food and raising chickens in their backyards, riding bikes and taking public transportation in place of using cars, and risking their freedom in order to stop practices destructive to both the environment and humanity, such as frac sand mining or nuclear weapons manufacturing. Catholic Workers are at the same time looking to decrease their dependence on oil and increase their capacity to live precariously among the least. They tend to the immediate needs of the body while maintaining a deeper connection to the rhythms of the earth. Of course, not every community does all of this perfectly—each has its own particular strengths and focus—but we learn from each other and support one another in deepening and strengthening our individual practices.

Many Catholic Worker communities, including us at New Hope, have begun to embrace the principles of permaculture, which we believe makes an important contribution towards acknowledging the necessity of creating a holistic ethic regarding people and creation. Permaculture—short for permanent culture—seeks to implement and support designs that mimic natural ecosystems, ensuring that all of creation is rightly honored. Moreover, permaculture minimizes the need for outside energy inputs (including human labor), all the while creating the conditions for a true human-nature equilibrium.

One example of a permaculturally designed garden that we practice is called "the Three Sisters," an annual polyculture that includes corn, beans, and squash, which originated with the indigenous peoples of this country. Growing side by side, the corn acts as a natural trellis up which the beans can climb, while the beans store much-needed nitrogen in the soil for use by the corn. In between is planted squash, which acts as a ground cover and pest repellant. These plants, grown together instead of separately, utilize the functions of the other in order to reap a maximum benefit for themselves, while at the same time minimizing the amount of energy needed from humans or fossil fuels to grow. Together, the three nourish us with an organic, complete protein. Building a trellis for the beans, fertilizing the corn, mulching and weeding—that time can now be spent growing other food or pursuing spiritual and intellectual interests.

As another example, a house designed along permacultural lines in a colder climate like our own would include south-facing windows that allow the sun's heat in during the winter, though not during the summer, so as to warm the house when necessary with fewer additional energy inputs such as using fossil fuels. These designs—and there are many, many more[8]—while quite simple, help illustrate the purpose of permaculture: to benefit humans while also benefitting creation.

During a recent permaculture course held here at New Hope Farm, our facilitator asked the participants to look out over a beautiful pasture

8. For an excellent introduction to permaculture and a variety of strategies, see Hemenway, *Gaia's Garden*.

35

that abutted a wooded hillside and to design a human homestead for it, utilizing concepts found within permaculture. One person in the class remarked that the landscape was "so perfect as it was, why not leave it alone? Why ruin it through human 'interference'?" Our facilitator reminded us that as permaculturalists, we are looking to allow *all* of the created world to flourish; and since humans are a part of the created world, we, too, need to flourish.

From a Christian perspective, I would assert that permaculture should be described as a way of designing a space so that everything in that space, whether living or nonliving, is able to reach the fullness of its intended purpose as given by God. Permaculture theory and design help us see more fully the reality of the interdependence of humans and the created world. When creation falters, so too will humanity, for as St. Paul says, the salvation of one is bound up in the salvation of the other. Conversely, when creation flourishes, so too will humanity—and then maybe, just maybe, we could proclaim with Sister Regina that God is indeed the life of all living.

4

Isn't All of Creation Violent?

Nekeisha Alexis-Baker

On August 17, 2012, *The Elkhart Truth* featured a story on efforts by Culver Duck Farms, one of North America's largest producers and suppliers of duck products, to become more environmentally friendly. As plant manager Tim McLaughlin explained, the industrial operation will "use the duck parts that don't make it to the dinner plate to help power the facility."[1] This task will involve creating generator fuel via on-site "recycling" of "all the waste and by-products [the facility] generates, *including the duck offal—blood and innards.*"[2] As I read the article, several questions immediately arose. How did 3.5 million slaughtered ducks per year come to be seen as a "renewable energy"? Aren't there ways to cut carbon emissions that are beneficial to the planet *and* to the ducks? Who determines what members of creation deserve protection, and why are these ducks excluded? Culver's greening model illustrates the dissonance that frequently surrounds the language and practice of creation care. Too often, people see sparing the lives of the animals routinely used for food strictly as an animal rights concern instead of an ecological one.

1. Vandenack, "Offal Will Help Fuel Middlebury Duck Farm."
2. Ibid. Emphasis mine.

On the one hand, more and more people are concerned about climate change, decry environmental degradation, and defend endangered plant and animal species. Christian consciousness around these problems has also grown as more theological and biblical resources on our responsibility to God's creation become available. Yet, many of these same Christians see calls to live compassionately with ducks, cows, chickens, pigs, and other "food" animals as misguided at best and antithetical to the gospel at worst. Even in the peace-loving circles of which I am a part, Christians are more likely to advocate eating flesh foods from less industrial ("humane") sources than to abstain from them altogether. Although veganism and vegetarianism are becoming more widespread, the number of Christians who embrace either practice remains small. That so few people, Christian or otherwise, incorporate a veg lifestyle into their greening efforts is surprising in light of the link between flesh-food production and some of the planet's most devastating environmental problems. Why is there so much resistance to a plant-based diet when eating less or no animal-based food whenever possible is more sustainable and considering that nonhuman animals are themselves valued members of God's creation?[3]

Although I have encountered many arguments against vegetarianism and veganism, one in particular is reflected in the question for this chapter. For some Christians, the fact of death and predation within nature makes it difficult to imagine not killing and eating the animals we call food. As my friend Autumn Brown put it in our exchange on this topic, "My environmental belief . . . is that death is a critically important part of ecology. My spiritual belief is that death is a part of the sacred process of creation that cannot and should not be forestalled. I believe that the death of any living thing is sacred, and in particular that the death of that living thing for the purpose of feeding another living thing is a sacrifice."[4] In this perspective, rearing, killing, and eating nonhuman animals is integral to a holy life-and-death cycle, and giving up flesh foods denies our place in the ecological chain. Since our current

3. For my previous writing on the importance of nonhuman animals in the biblical tradition, see my "Doesn't the Bible Say that Humans Are More Important than Animals?"

4. See "Food as Spiritual and Political Praxis 2."

environmental predicament is due in part to humanity's refusal to live humbly with creation, some proponents of responsible meat, dairy, and egg consumption see using other animals for food as essential to a holistic relationship with creation. From this vantage point, nonviolence toward other animals is an unattainable and even questionable goal.

On the surface, this argument reflects a kind of common sense. All one has to do is look out the window or spend a few hours watching the new *Animal Planet* to see how ruthless nature can be. But is it the case that suffering and violence in creation necessarily prevents human attempts to live peaceably with our animal kin? Is orienting our lives toward nonviolence through vegetarianism and veganism truly an unrealistic or undesirable goal? Although it might seem strange to respond to the question "Isn't all creation violent?" with an argument about eating, I hear this question most when I promote abstaining from flesh foods as an integral part of peacemaking with creation. Therefore, I will start by engaging two of the assumptions behind the question and reflect on the possibility—and even the necessity—of using a plant-based diet to live well with the earth and its inhabitants.

Wrestling with Underlying Assumptions

Eating Other Animals Is the Way to Participate in Creation's Life-Death Cycle

No one can escape nature's ongoing saga of death and life. Everyone—including the most compassionate, fair-trade-buying, vegan locavore—harms other creatures. Suffering and death occur unintentionally as beings of different sizes, shapes, abilities, and levels of power interact with each other. For every nonhuman animal I care for and leave off the menu, there are innumerable others whom I unwittingly kill and who die in the process of producing the plant-based foods I eat. Suffering and death are also biological necessities. Cheetahs hunt and kill gazelles to feed their cubs. Ants kill and dissect other insects for their colony. Chimpanzee bands occasionally attack and eat smaller primates. From microbes to mammals, creatures feed upon one another for sustenance, for survival, and even for sport.

In light of predatory violence, everyday meat-eaters and conscientious omnivores alike dismiss as naïve vegan and vegetarian attempts to live peaceably with creation. Indeed, veg-living is often described as a futile attempt at death avoidance, a temptation that is "akin to the Gnostic tendency to deny the incarnation in all its embodied and fleshly character, and the cross of Jesus Christ" and "a refusal to accept creation on God's terms."[5] However, I contend that it is precisely because life and death are so thoroughly interconnected in creation that consuming other animals and their by-products without ecological, biological, or geographical imperatives to do so lacks a strong ethical basis.

If all creatures feed on each other continuously, then what is the rationale for gratuitously killing *more* animals? Or, asked differently, if nature is already "red in tooth and claw," then what (or whose) purpose is really being served by using more violence to satisfy a dietary preference or philosophical outlook?[6] Meat-eaters, including the "conscious carnivores"[7] pursuing a more visceral connection to their flesh foods, rarely engage such questions. Since death is an inextricable part of eating, one would imagine that "conscious herbivorism" would also be a powerful emerging movement. After all, all humans must eat plants to live, and plant-based foods are arguably more accessible to more people when compared to foods from animals that are locally raised, organically grown, compassionately treated, *and* "humanely" killed.[8] Yet these

---

5. Wirzba, *Food and Faith*, 135.

6. The phrase "Nature, red in tooth and claw" comes from Alfred Lord Tennyons's poem "In Memoriam A. H. H.," canto 56. Interestingly, such a notion of "nature" served to replace older notions of "Mother Nature," a feminine figure whose nurture and care is necessary for life, with a demonic image. On this see Adams, "Woman Red in Tooth and Claw."

7. "Conscious carnivores" is a recent term adopted by human omnivores who eat flesh foods from less industrial sources—usually small, local farms—and who participate in the meat-making process by sourcing the origins of the animal, butchering the animal bodies themselves, and/or deliberately watching as others kill the animals for them. For one example of the movement, see Cole, "Conscious Carnivores, Ethical Butchers."

8. Flesh-food eaters often claim that plant-based eating is an elite and expensive diet to maintain. Although it is true that specialty and niche vegan and vegetarian foods can strain one's budget, a diet based on whole foods (fruits, vegetables, grains, etc.) need not be costly. Ironically, the very practices adopted by conscious carnivores,

days, one is more likely to hear stories of people exploring the sacredness of life and death by slaughtering an overpowered animal or watching unflinchingly as someone else does the butchering than by decapitating a head of broccoli or planting a vegetable garden.[9] This discrepancy leaves me wondering: Are these experiments in taking another animal's life for food about valuing creation more deeply? Or are these acts of intimate violence an extension of our society's preoccupation with bloodshed and self-gratification? Is sentimental flesh-food eating primarily about participating in nature's complex web? Or has predation become a handy tool for justifying status quo eating habits and maintaining the dominant relationship between humans and other animals?[10]

It Is Natural for People to Eat Other Animals

In an article directed to veg-identified readers, journalist Mark Bittman addressed the issue of killing animals for food when it isn't necessary, saying, "The defense is this: it may be inhumane, but it isn't un-human.

---

such as eating grass-fed beef and learning to slaughter other animals, can be more costly and less accessible to the average eater than adopting and maintaining a plant-based diet.

9. For a few stories, see Sellers, "Mark Zuckerberg's New Challenge"; Dailey, "The Conscious Carnivore"; and Kaminer, "The Main Course Had an Unhappy Face . . ."

10. I am always intrigued by the way self-proclaimed "conscious carnivores" tend to describe their experience of killing other animals. The narrative is often movielike in its tone, with elements of tension, high drama, release, and happy resolution. There is initial nervousness at "doing it right" so as not to cause "too much" pain; details about wielding the weapon, holding the animal down, cutting the animal's throat and feeling his or her life slip away; remorseless gratitude as the animal's body is served and eaten; and finally, the bonus feature—the animal's flesh tastes better, too! Yet, authors rarely reflect with any sophistication on what their actions mean for the animals themselves. Besides the obligatory mention that slaughterhouses cause more suffering, which apparently excuses the suffering that *is* caused by unnecessary intimate violence, there is little consideration for the animals' experience: their feelings, their loss, their desire to live, their purpose independent of the human will being exercised over them. Why do experiments aimed at fostering a stronger connection to animals used as food produce accounts that remain so anthropocentric, individualistic, and self-absorbed in nature? Can committing the ultimate act of dominance over another living being out of curiosity and self-interest truly inspire people to live more humbly with and in creation?

It's traditional. It's mainstream, and almost everyone alive who can eat meat does so."[11] Bittman does not explain the rationale behind his response in any depth. However, others who share a similar outlook often turn to paleontology, biology, and other scientific disciplines to demonstrate that "humans have evolved for the past two millions years as omnivorous hunters/gatherers and have as much right to eat meat as any other predator on this planet."[12] Unsurprisingly, the idea that humans have evolutionary grounds to eat other animals is highly contested by those who assert that humans are behavioral omnivores who primarily eat flesh foods out of habit, not physiological need. Several thousand years ago, Platonist philosopher Plutarch made this claim, saying, "A man's frame is in no way similar to those creatures who were made for flesh-eating; he has no hooked beak or sharp nails or jagged teeth, no strong stomach or warmth of vital fluids able to digest and assimilate a heavy diet of flesh. It is from this very fact . . . that Nature disavows our eating of flesh."[13]

But in my view, debating whether or not eating meat is a human birthright is beside the point. We know with certainty that humans are not carnivores who have no choice but to eat other animals. Furthermore, we do not have to base our eating practices on prehistoric times any more than we base our other ethics and discernment solely on the practices of hominids. As Christian, vegan, and animal advocate Bruce Friedrich writes, "Eating meat may be 'natural,' and most humans may find it acceptable—humans certainly have been doing it for a very long time—but these are not moral arguments. . . . The law of the jungle is not a moral standard, however much it may make meat eaters feel better about their meat eating."[14] Regardless of what our early ancestors ate, our ecological situation today demands that we make decisions in light of our present crisis and our hopes for a more sustainable future.

11. Bittman, "Eating Meat Is Only Human."

12. Powlesland, "Eating Meat Is Natural." As an aside, the "conscious carnivore" movement appears to also be an attempt to show that flesh-food eating is an inherent part of the human experience by adopting the same posture that true carnivores have for their prey, namely becoming adept at killing and eating other animals without squeamishness or reservation.

13. Plutarch, "On the Eating of Flesh," 551.

14. Quoted in Foer, *Eating Animals*, 213.

We must examine how what we put in our mouths affects the world around us and ask whether it leads to unnecessary cruelty, violence, and destruction, or to greater compassion, a deeper appreciation for life, and a more harmonious relationship with the only creation we and our nonhuman neighbors know.

Facing the Reality

People Must Limit Their Consumption of Flesh Foods
for Creation to Survive

Today, factory farming is responsible for at least 40 percent of the total flesh-food production worldwide, including 74 percent of all poultry, 50 percent of all pork, 43 percent of all beef, and 68 percent of all eggs.[15] In the United States, the numbers are much more staggering, as this system produces 99.9 percent of chickens raised for meat, 97 percent of laying hens, 99 percent of turkeys, 95 percent of pigs, and 78 percent of cattle.[16] In this model of flesh-food production, humans use technological prowess to manipulate other animals' instinctual, biological, and social traits to our benefit, at their expense. The abuses these creatures suffer from standard industry practices as well as from wanton cruelty at the hands of underpaid, stressed, and mistreated workers are too numerous to catalog here. However, if you can imagine pregnant sows forced into crates so small they cannot turn around; hormone-injected dairy cows who develop udder infections from producing abnormally high amounts of milk; egg-laying hens with mutilated beaks who live out their days in a space no bigger than a regular sheet of paper; male chicks, useless to the egg-laying industry, being suffocated in plastic garbage bags at hatcheries; and turkeys bred to be so large that they can no longer reproduce naturally or carry their own weight, you will catch a tiny glimpse of the unrelenting horrors these animals undergo because of the human demand for flesh foods.

In addition to their physical suffering, farmed animals in this system endure psychological and emotional distress due to "the daily

15. Nierenberg, *Happier Meals*, 5, 11–12.
16. Foer, *Eating Animals*, 109.

traumas of confinement, overcrowding, perpetual exposure to respiratory irritants, digestive unrest from supplemented feed, lethargy from unnaturally rapid weight gain, and the aggressive behavior of other stressed animals."[17] The nonstop agony continues until the animals leave their cages long enough to be packed into trucks and transported to slaughterhouses, where they are beaten, dragged, stunned, and mutilated until they finally find peace in death. Industrial animal agriculture even extends to the sea. Longline fishing kills 145 non-target fish and other species annually, including 3.3 million sharks, 1 million marlins, 60,000 sea turtles, 75,000 albatross, and 20,000 dolphins and whales.[18] Meanwhile, shrimp trawlers trap hundreds of additional species who are then "crushed together, gashed on corals, bashed on rocks—for hours—and then hauled from the water, causing painful decompression (the decompression sometimes causes the animals' eyes to pop out or their internal organs to come out of their mouths)."[19] At all times, industrial animal agriculture prevents other animals from living in ways that God created them to be. To excuse this unfettered annihilation of other creatures as part of our evolutionary destiny or the "natural" life-and-death cycle is to have a limited and distorted view of human nature and of God's creation.

If farmed animals are the primary victims in the animal agriculture system, the rest of creation is collateral damage. Today, grazing uses more than 26 percent of the earth's ice-free surfaces, with more than 33 percent of arable land dedicated to growing feed crops and more than 70 percent of the Amazon forest reserved for animal pastures. In addition, the industry uses 8 percent of human water sources for irrigation, threatening human health and safety as unpolluted fresh water sources become scarcer, and produces at least 18 percent of greenhouse gas emissions—more than the amount produced by transportation.[20]

17. Halteman, "Varieties of Harm to Animals in Industrial Farming," 125.

18. Foer, *Eating Animals*, 191.

19. Ibid., 192.

20. *Livestock's Long Shadow*, xxi, xxii, 5. Eighteen percent of greenhouse gas emissions may be an underestimation, according to a more recent report from the Worldwatch Institute, which claims that up to 51 percent of greenhouse gas emissions are related to livestock production. See Goodland and Anhang, "Livestock and Climate Change."

As the livestock industry has expanded globally, it continues to create major increases in deforestation, overgrazing, compacted soil, soil erosion, and rapid decline in wildlife biodiversity. It remains a primary source of water pollution, coastal "dead" zones, coral reef degradation, and the emergence of antibiotic resistance. In an effort to respond to these ecological disasters, agribusinesses are seeking solutions through biotechnology. Instead of admitting this massive system has failed other animals and creation, and scaling back these operations to drastically reduce their impact, the industry presses on with fixes such as modifying pig genes with mice chromosomes to create less toxic manure, engineering dairy cows to be more resistant to mastitis, and using duck bodies as generator fuel.[21]

Humane Farming Is a Good Start, but Preserving Creation Will Require More

One consumer response to factory farming's stranglehold on the environment is to purchase flesh foods from more compassionate and ecologically sustainable alternatives. Consequently, there has been a slow but noticeable increase in "humane" farms and in the number of people who buy from these sources. While the movement for less industrial farming is more idyllic and eco friendly in many ways, it has its share of pitfalls. First, there is the practice of greenwashing whereby companies brand their flesh foods as "grass fed," "cage free," and "free range," despite continuing some of the same abuses. A free-range chicken farm may still house thirty thousand hens in a dark shed as long as there is a nearby door that occasionally opens to a small patch of dirt. Thousands of grass-fed cows may still be confined to tiny stalls and die in a typical slaughterhouse; they just happen to eat piles of cut grass instead of grain. Second, there are routine problems associated with raising animals for food, even if the animals are on a less industrial farm. Happy dairy cows still undergo artificial insemination, spend their days producing milk for humans, and are denied the chance to nurse and rear their young. In the case of egg production, the hatcheries that grind male chicks alive because they are useless to the egg-laying industry also supply

21. Nierenberg, *Happier Meals*, 52–53.

hens to factory farms and to the backyards of conscientious omnivores alike. Third, due to U.S. Department of Agriculture regulations, many "humane" farmers must still send their animals to the same horrific slaughterhouses as their factory-farmed peers. A steer can spend his days living painlessly on an organic farm and nevertheless experience torture at the time of death.[22]

One example of the ways "humane" farms can still be tied to the industrial system is Polyface Farms, touted by the popular writer Michael Pollan and by Duke ethicist Norman Wirzba.[23] Polyface, which is located in Virginia's Shenandoah Valley, is a pasture-based operation. Its owners call the farm a "clean meat connection"[24] thanks to standard practices like allowing cows and pigs to forage within portable electric fencing; letting chickens live in fields where they receive fresh air, sunshine, and exercise; and raising turkeys in outdoor hoop houses. For some sentimental flesh-food eaters, such as Wirzba, Polyface demonstrates "that our production of food . . . can serve to promote the dance of creation, and so bring praise and glory and thanksgiving to our lips and glory to God."[25] Yet Polyface still uses turkeys and chickens that were selectively bred for the industrial system. The turkeys still cannot reproduce on their own, and all the birds grow at an unnaturally rapid rate and are killed weeks after their birth. Some of the same contradictions are also apparent on a less industrial operation like Niman Ranch. On farms that do business with Niman Ranch, animals forage, socialize, live outdoors, and engage in other species-relevant behaviors. Yet farmers still brand their cattle, castrate day-old pigs without anesthesia, and transport the animals long distances to die in slaughterhouses.[26] In each of these instances, the animals lived in vastly better conditions than their factory-farmed counterparts. But being reared with significantly less suffering does not guarantee protection from unnecessary cruelty, nor does it allow consumers to opt out of the industrial system.

22. Foer, *Eating Animals*, 197.
23. See Pollan, *Omnivore's Dilemma*, 125–31, and Wirzba, "Barnyard Dance."
24. See the Web site of Polyface, Inc.: http://www.polyfacefarms.com/.
25. Wirzba, "Barnyard Dance," 9.
26. Foer, *Eating Animals*, 168, 197.

The same conundrum arises when considering the interplay between less-industrial flesh-food production and care for the environment. On the one hand, "humane," local, and organic animal farms pollute significantly less than factory farm alternatives. However, ruminant animals still produce methane, a gas that is *23 times more potent than carbon dioxide,*[27] whether they are trapped in a stall or grazing in a pasture. In the United States alone, dairy and beef cattle emit approximately 5.5 million metric tons of methane annually, accounting for 20 percent of the nation's methane emissions. Globally, animals like sheep, buffalo, and goats are already producing about 80 million metric tons each year. Methane pollution from animal agriculture is such a threat that Dr. Rajendra Pachauri, chair of the United Nations Intergovernmental Panel on Climate Change and a vegetarian, has urged people—especially those living in the Western world—to eat less meat. Breeding more cows, pigs, ducks, and other animals to support the desire for flesh foods instead of increasing the demand for less intensive plant-based alternatives simply does not make sense given the environmental situation the world is now in.[28]

When compared to factory farming, less industrial operations can connect the eater to the life-and-death cycle, provide a better life for animals until the point of slaughter, use less technological power over other animals, and do less harm to the environment. However, this system is more likely to *supplement* instead of supplant the dominant farming model, especially if advocates of the "humane" option are inconsistent in their practice. As author of *Happier Meals* Danielle Nierenberg cautions, "Ultimately, we, as consumers, will have to reconsider the place of meat in our diets. Reversing the human health and environmental problems caused by our appetite for modern meat will by necessity mean eating fewer animal products."[29] People must reduce the socioeconomic power of flesh foods because an overall growth of flesh-food production—both industrial and "humane"—will be *more* taxing on creation, not less.

27. Jowit, "UN Says Eat Less Meat." Emphasis added. Carbon dioxide is the gas most commonly associated with climate change.

28. Hall, "Sustainable, Free-Range Farms."

29. Nierenberg, *Happier Meals*, 65–66.

Conclusion

Is creation violent? The short answer is yes. But our response need not end there. Although creation contains violence that is necessary for life, it also contains violence that is unwarranted and preventable. Pointing to our carnivorous animal neighbors to excuse factory farms or to microbes in the soil as justification for decimating our oceans is counterintuitive at best and reckless at worst. The existence of death and suffering in the life cycle does not negate vegan and vegetarian attempts at peacemaking with other animals, including limiting the use of gratuitous violence against them, showing them compassion, and valuing them as friends, neighbors, and kin. Predation in the natural world does not preclude people from opting out of farming and killing systems that dehumanize workers, produce mass cruelty, and cause unspeakable environmental harm. What our prehuman ancestors ate does not inhibit humanity's ability to reconcile with inanimate creation by giving up sentimental attachments to flesh and other foods that threaten the earth's very existence, even if the source of those products eases our consciences. It is up to those of us who are able to make changes—especially those of us who have been most responsible for the world's current ecological outlook—to do everything we can for the sake of other animals and the planet as a whole. Plant-based eating is one of those crucial steps, and for this reason it should not be overlooked.

5

Should We Intervene to Conserve Biodiversity?
A Brief (and Timid) Defense of Zoological Gardens

Tripp York

> I have heard nearly as much nonsense about zoos as I have
> about God and religion.
>
> —Yann Martel, *Life of Pi*

I'M OCCASIONALLY ASKED, "WHY is a professor of religious studies shoveling elephant and giraffe poop on the weekends?" For me, the answer is in the question, but let me provide a little context.

A few years ago I taught a seminar called "Living Lives that Matter." I was probably the least qualified person on campus to teach it. To be honest, I have no idea why they asked me to teach it. It's not that I don't think I have lived, thus far, an interesting life; I just don't think I have lived a life that, in the grand scheme of things, actually matters.

Maybe that's okay. Maybe there is some sense by which Christian claims about time and resurrection liberate us from the notion that our lives *have* to matter—or, at least, matter in some sense that we can name them as historically significant.

As I said, I don't know why I was asked to teach the course, but I jumped at the opportunity. I was fortunate to have a bright group of students working through questions like the following: "Are some lives more significant than others?" "What does work have to do with what it means to be human?" "What does a meaningful life look like?" "What does religion, love, death, work, politics, family, and friendship have to do with living a life that matters?"

As you can well imagine, it was the kind of class that needed to be longer than one semester.

We spent the majority of our time reading as many people as I could conceivably fit into one semester. We examined biographies, essays, novels, short stories, and plays. We read everyone from Homer to Emma Goldman, from Aung San Suu Kyi to Will Eisner. Actually, the main problem with the class was that all we did was read. In retrospect, a little less reading and a little more doing would have been helpful.

In my normal attempt to indoctrinate my students on those matters I find important (after all, professors should profess), I included a section on wildlife conservation. Initially, this struck a number of my students as quite odd. After all, when it comes to life's "big questions," doesn't it make more sense to read Aristotle, St. Paul, and Shakespeare? Why bother reading Annie Dillard's take on weasels or learning why Clem Coetsee stressed the importance of dehorning rhinos? Indeed, when surrounded by the safe concrete walls of the university (where the only nature students typically encounter is in a biology lab), such readings did seem to be a bit of a stretch.

Nevertheless, as we started to examine some of the complex and oftentimes contradictory saints of the wildlife conservation movement, such as Helen Freeman, Dian Fossey, Lawrence Anthony, and Steve Irwin, my students began gravitating to the vision that these conservationists shared. This process was due not to any verbal arguments made by these activists; rather, my students found these activists compelling because of the tangibility of their lives. What these conservationists did, what they contributed to the world and how they lived, was so utterly concrete. Whether it was Fossey's fight for the gorillas, Anthony's relationships with elephants, Freeman's unparalleled work with snow leopards, or the eccentric passion that drove Irwin to fall madly in love with crocodiles, my students were moved by their ability to live life passionately—as if it were a gift. Though there was much my students disagreed with in the lives and writings of these individuals, they were all impressed by the fact that they at least lived lives worthy of discussion. That, in and of itself, is an achievement.

Of course, I don't think any of these people lived the way they lived just to provoke a discussion. I think they did it, at the risk of sounding reductionist, because of their convictions about the purpose of human existence. In this sense, the way they lived was their best argument for how they viewed the good that is creation. Their lives also say something about what it means to live meaningfully without having to slide into pure relativism. For their lives assumed the kind of purpose that directly said something about what it means not only to be human, but to be here as a gift. Finding such lives worthy of conversation remains, I think, a theological imperative.

While people like Sojourner Truth and Malcolm X were obvious theological choices for discussion in the course, we discovered that the witness of folks like Fossey and Anthony required us to reimagine what it means to live well among the millions of other species that Christians claim are the work of God. We found ourselves wondering why wildlife conservation was such a consistently ignored topic in the field of Christian ethics. For a body of people quick to say that creation is good, we do not seem to spend much time living as if creation is good. How can we live meaningful lives that are also mindful lives? How do we live doxologically ordered lives that see the chief end of *all* existence as communion with God? On that score, doesn't the preservation of animals become not only an ecological necessity but also a theological one?

A Shipwrecked Ark

> I don't mean to defend zoos. Close them all down if you
> want (and let us hope that what wildlife remains can sur-
> vive in what is left of the natural world).
>
> —Yann Martel, *Life of Pi*

Fast-forward a year later and I find myself working through such questions by serving as a Keeper Aide in the Virginia Zoological Park in Norfolk, Virginia. Of course, my fascination with rhinos, sloths, and squirrel monkeys may have played a significant role in my decision to serve as a Keeper Aide as well, but I've always been interested in how zoos can function, metaphorically and literally, as both an ark and a garden. In doing so, they have the potential to provide a corrective lens against apathy toward nonhuman life.

Many people are rightly divided on the subject of zoos, and zoos certainly have had a tumultuous history (which may be putting it lightly). Though this is not the place to try to give a history of zoological gardens, what we do know of them suggests that they may have originated approximately five thousand years ago. We know that King Shulgia (2094–2047 BCE) of Mesopotamia kept a number of "exotic" creatures, and that Queen Hatshepsut, of the eighteenth dynasty, was responsible for the first recorded animal collecting expedition (around 1490 BCE).[1] From the ancient Egyptians to Chinese and Roman Emperors, the housing of exotics was often practiced for a variety of reasons: respect and awe of nature, religious belief and piety, display of power and wealth as well as scientific investigation. The showcasing of animals, for whatever reason, has a long and varied history that, in many ways, culminates in the modern zoo.

Zoos today, at least the ones accredited by the American Zoo and Aquarium Association, boast an emphasis on conservation and education. The modern zoo attempts to achieve a number of goals, including the protection of genetic resources (which makes breeding and release programs possible), financially contributing to wildlife conservation and field research, and, most importantly, functioning as a school of public education that teaches its visitors the importance of biodiversity.

What is of particular interest to me is how zoos can serve to function as a good for all animals and how that good can be adjudicated amidst the tension of displaying nonhuman animals for the entertainment of human animals. After all, the large contribution that zoos directly make toward conservation and education is not possible if nobody pays to see the animals. The chief tension that many conscientious keepers, curators, and zoo directors have to negotiate is one between natural habitats and good exhibits. A good exhibit often makes for a bad habitat, and a good habitat often makes for a bad exhibit. Many animals naturally

1. Croke, *Modern Ark*, 129.

retreat from the presence of humans, so zoos do everything they can to give animals a place to hide from the public eye. Of course, zoo visitors do not pay to see animals in "retreat." Providing an adequate habitat and satisfying visitors' curiosity is a balancing act. Good zoos show absolute care and concern for each individual animal, while being aware that if the animals are not visible to the public then the zoos will not remain in business for very long. For some people, the fact that many of these animals prefer to retreat from the human eye may be their principal argument *against* zoos!

Such a sentiment, however, betrays a very naïve understanding of zoos, the wild, and how the two do and do not conflict. Many of the animals in zoos were not captured from that blissful place called "the wild" that some people still imagine to exist. Such an idea betrays a lack of knowledge of what sorts of free spaces do and do not exist, and what (and how many) animals can successfully live in them. For example, many elephants that are in zoos were either captive-bred or rescued from the closest thing we have to something once considered to be the wild. The process of culling has been one of the key factors to placing elephants in zoos. I was recently in a conversation with an animal rights advocate (we live six blocks from PETA's world headquarters, which, in turn, is only two miles from the zoo) who was trying to convince me of how superior the life of our African elephants would be in Africa as opposed to Norfolk. I agreed. I think most of the people working in zoos would also agree, if not for one thing: there is no place in Africa for them to return to. Many of the elephants we have in the United States were not, as discussed above, "kidnapped" from the wild; rather, they were rescued from wildlife parks that, for the sake of that particular ecosystem (including endangered species), practice culling.[2] What many people fail to understand is that much of Africa has a fence around it. What

2. Outside of humans, elephants have the ability to drastically alter and destroy their environments. Conservationists in wildlife parks started the process of culling as a means of keeping the numbers of elephants down so that other species—the black rhino, for instance—would have a chance at survival. Due to the work of folks such as Lawrence Anthony, many parks are now attempting to employ birth control as opposed to culling. Either way you go, it is intervention. Birth control is a lot more expensive than culling, which demands that those who are opposed to culling be a part of the process of figuring out how to raise money for the birth control.

exists there are various African parks. Nearly everything is managed. There is no wild left to which to return. The occasional visitor to the zoo who bemoans the supposed plight of our captive (enslaved? rescued? both?) animals often imagines an Edenic African wild that just happens to be hospitable to all living creatures and has not been encroached upon by humans. Such an idea is groundless. Such land does not exist. Even if we could, to stay with the example of elephants, send them back "home," where would we send them? Their populations are tightly managed in parks, which is how, outside of captive-bred elephants, many zoos ended up with elephants in the first place. It is not as if zoos are sending people to Africa (and Asia) to kidnap elephants. They often come to North America because there is nowhere else for them to go. Simply put, these elephants would be killed in the very places many zoo opponents falsely imagine to be free from us humans. This is why those animal rights organizations that demand that we "not intervene" are, quite possibly, living on another planet.[3] Nonintervention is impossible. We intervene constantly (even when we are not aware of it). Whether it is the farmlands that feed us while disrupting the homes of groundhogs, the clear-cutting of forests that spells disaster and extinction for countless animals, the building of roads, tunnels, and bridges that displace innumerable creatures, the inadvertent burying of gopher tortoises under construction lots in Florida, or the poaching of rhinos and elephants throughout Africa, we are constantly intervening. There is no "hands-off" approach. The question is not whether we are going to intervene, but *how* do we intervene?

This is where zoos, along with other conservation-based entities, can be a good thing. I have conversed with zoo directors, curators, keepers, wildlife conservationists, and biologists of all stripes, and the one thing they almost all agree about is that there is little hope for ani-

---

3. When zoos in both San Diego and Tampa rescued a number of elephants from execution in Swaziland, many animal rights advocates argued it would be better for the elephants to be systematically executed than to live a life of captivity. Without even responding to the pure self-righteousness and hubris one must assume to declare another animal is better riddled with bullets than living in a zoo, I can honestly say that, in visiting some of these elephants, seeing their habitats, their daily enrichment, their diets, and their relationships with zoo staff, that such "advocates" are wrong. For more information, see French, *Zoo Story*, 1–21.

mals remaining in the wild. This is not pessimism. There is simply little hope left for our land. It is not going to reemerge, and as the old saying goes, "God's not making any more of it." Most of it is gone, and what is not protected and managed is quickly disappearing. Due to the loss of natural habitats, zoos (alongside sanctuaries) are becoming one of the few remaining options we have for preserving what is left. Until the wholesale destruction of ecosystems comes to a halt, I am not sure that there is any hope left for them in their native environments. So, in terms of the sordid history of zoos, the question is not so much what they were doing last century, or even a decade ago, but what are they doing now? Can they become the kinds of places that practice hospitality to those animals in need? Can they offer something that is quickly becoming absent in this world? That is, can they be a good home for animals that are losing their homes?

Pulling Weeds

> I have amazing news for you. Man is not alone on this planet. He is part of a community, upon which he depends absolutely.
>
> – Daniel Quinn, *Ishmael*

The above questions are in a constant state of negotiation, and I cannot answer them. Over the past few years, I have spent a significant amount of time behind the scenes at several zoos discussing these very issues with curators, keepers, and zoo directors. I have conversed with private owners of everything from elephants to green tree pythons, and also with circus workers and members of PETA. I have spent the last year and a half working in a zoo with everything from tamanduas to screaming hairy armadillos. I can say that I have learned that when it comes to zoos, it is not a black-and-white issue. I've seen the good, and I've seen the bad. I've seen the *really* good, and I've seen the *really* bad. The reactions that zoos elicit from people are as varied as the animals within them. Zoos can inspire people to become wildlife conservationists; they can also inspire people to see animals as nothing more than exotic entertainment—as mere commodities to be visually consumed.

Zoos have habitats that are too small and habitats that, believe it or not, are too large. Often the habitats are purely artificial and designed more with the viewer in mind than the one being viewed. Animals in zoos are often traded at whim to fit whatever niche is demanded from one zoo to the next. Some of the animals will never thrive in these environments, and while some animals live longer in zoos, others do not. There are also quality of life concerns. Most animals in zoos are better fed than animals in the wild, but at what cost?[4] At the risk of sounding anthropomorphic (what other language can I possibly use?), some of the animals in zoos are miserable, just as I imagine some of the animals in the wild are miserable. At the same time, some of the animals in zoos are happy, just as I imagine some animals in the wild are happy. So, as an animal advocate, I find myself trying to pull resources from both proponents *and* opponents of zoos in an attempt to find a realistic solution that takes into consideration the vast complexity behind the problem of vanishing and captive species. We have to ask ourselves basic questions about not only why animals are in captivity, but how our theological convictions about them have both led to their captivity (necessity or otherwise) and how their placement in zoos continues to shape our perspective of them.

Fortunately, many contemporary zoologists are practicing a direction based on careful scientifically motivated models of conservation. While zoos certainly do exist for entertainment, their primary purposes are education, conservation, and the protection of certain species from, ironically, us humans. Just as Noah built an ark to protect animals from God's punishment, we now build arks in order to protect animals from *human* punishment. In some cases, zoos are the only places left where animals can even exist at all.[5]

The hope of such gardens (metaphorically reminiscent of Eden) is to embolden our imaginations so that we can faithfully embody the

4. "Better fed" may be a problematic way of putting it. Many zoos feed their animals so "well" that, like many North American humans, they're obese. Dieticians and nutritionists are beginning to play an important role in zoos, ensuring that the animals are as healthy as possible.

5. From Partula snails to Micronesian Kingfishers, there are more than thirty species of animals that exist only in zoos. Due to the diligence of conservationists and their breeding programs, including the breeding and release program of bongos we have at our own zoo, some of these are actually making a comeback in wildlife parks.

very claims we make about the good that is creation. Just as Isaiah 11 presents a compelling image of the original peace restored, these gardens have the potential to offer a glimpse of this reality. In making such a claim I am certainly not trying to romanticize zoo culture; I am only suggesting that, placing the many convoluted issues about them aside, they are symbolic of our estrangement from, and our eschatological connection to, the rest of creation. As with the lives of our eccentric ecological saints, zoos remind us that, despite our culture's incessant need to spiritualize the material, creation really does matter. They remind us that all of life is a gift: a gift that can be touched, respected, and enjoyed, or one that can be—and often is—abused, ignored, and neglected.

So part of the reason why I spend my weekends shoveling poop at the zoo is simply because zoos (and poop) exist. Zoos have the capability to become (and, in many ways, already are) a symbol of humanity's attempt to save what we have tried to destroy. They are living photographs of what we are losing. They are gardens with weeds, shipwrecked arks, and mountains where wolves live with sheep.

6

Caring for Orphans: An Experiment in Interspecies Care at Noah's Ark in Georgia

L. Diane Smith

DREAMS SOMETIMES SUDDENLY EXPLODE into being, but more often they start small—as a mere seed, waiting to grow. This is the story of one particular person's dream coinciding with the vision given in Isaiah: "The wolf shall live with the lamb, the leopard will lie down with the kid, the calf and the lion and the fatling together, and a little child shall lead them" (Isa 11:6). At age four, Jama Connor knew that she wanted to "help all the animals that nobody wants." She wanted to live the peaceable kingdom.

Of course, simply having a pet or rescuing the local bedraggled cat was not going to be enough for this youngster. She knew she had to save all things in need, which complicated the itinerant lifestyle of her family. Her parents, Leonard and Louella Connor, were traveling evangelists. The motels and rentals in which they stayed often did not allow animals. Undeterred, Jama found a way to sneak animals in need into their room. On more than one occasion her family was asked to leave once the duplicity was discovered by motel staff.

The Connors were certainly not a wealthy family. They didn't have much money, and they often gave away more than they kept. As such, extras like taking four children to the zoo were generally not possible. As Jama began to realize this, she proclaimed, "When I *get* the animals, I will never charge anyone to see them." She would not allow lack of funds to prevent any child from seeing and experiencing the wonder and unconditional love of animals.

When Jama was a few years older she experienced a very harsh reality. The Connors were on a mission trip to Mexico and while there they visited an orphanage. Their impressionable daughter discovered that just as there are unwanted animals in this world, so there are many unwanted children. So, she added them to her dream.

Unlike many childhood dreams that are easily forgotten and abandoned, this one begged to be fulfilled. And so it was when, in 1990, Jama and her family (now the Hedgecoths) found a farm for sale in Locust Grove, Georgia. Though the animals did not come two by two, they did come to the farm, which would become known as Noah's Ark. Before long, the Ark housed two hundred animals and a handful of displaced children.

The Ark was perfect for the family's desire to care for the neglected. The cost, unfortunately, was more than they could afford. Jama had borrowed money for a down payment and promised to pay monthly installments. It was a promise she found difficult to keep. The family and its menagerie of animals faced eviction several times as the family fell further and further behind on the rent. Jama prayed a familiar prayer, "Lord, I'm in a mess again."

She called an attorney to see if there was any way around the eviction. The answer was no, they would have to vacate the premises in thirty days. The family gathered together and prayed. Then, the phone rang. It was the attorney calling back. He had mentioned her plight to a client who had the means to help. "He and his wife want to pay off your property," the attorney said. At the time, Jama had never met these generous people. Her affirmation that her vision of a peaceable kingdom ultimately belonged to God—not her—was substantiated.

While the property itself was large enough, the two-bedroom house that came with it was too small for the growing two- and four-legged family. The benefactors who had paid for the property added a house with ten bedrooms and ten bathrooms to their already substantial gift.

As their lodgings grew, it was time for things to become official. Noah's Ark had been "grandfathered in" with licensing to care for the animals following an inspection by the Department of Natural Resources and the U.S. Department of Agriculture. The inspectors found the animals so well cared for that they granted all needed licensing. The first exotic animal to arrive was an Asiatic black bear named Susie Q (who still lives at Noah's Ark).

In time, the animals and children needed more resources than the Hedgecoth family could provide. Dumpster diving was more commonplace than they wanted to admit—hungry mouths had to be fed. It was time to make a way for others to give and be blessed. Applications were sent to the Internal Revenue Service for 501(c)(3) nonprofit status for Noah's Ark Animal Rehabilitation Center, Inc., and Noah's Ark Children's Care Home, Inc. This made it possible for people to make tax-deductible donations that would help provide for the children and animals. Board members were put in place, and Jama Hedgecoth found herself the official founder and director of two full-fledged nonprofit organizations housed on one property.

The usual way of taking in children was to "find" the ones in need—whether by word of mouth or as castaways hiding behind a dumpster. This, too, needed the official stamp of approval, and Noah's Ark became licensed by the State of Georgia to provide basic residential care for foster children. The Georgia Department of Family and Children Services referred children to Noah's Ark, which averages sixteen children at a time, age birth to eighteen years old.

The children's stories resonated with their caregivers. While some had been neglected to the point that they did not understand the need for basic hygiene, like changing sheets and brushing their teeth, others came with deep scars from emotional, physical, and sexual abuse. Each child came hurting, frightened, and broken. And each one finally learned what it meant to be nurtured. Sibling groups could come together, maintaining as much of a feeling of family as possible.

Throughout the years, Noah's Ark has been home to over four hundred children. Most stayed an average of eighteen to twenty-four months, though many have stayed longer.

While the Ark has helped hundreds of children, the Noah's Ark family has rehabbed literally thousands of animals. Local wildlife (babies or wounded) are rehabilitated and then released into the wild. Farm animals come to live at Noah's Ark and dot the 250 acres in an odd combination of horses, goats, sheep, cows, pigs, llamas, emus, geese, and buffalo. Some have only one eye, others walk with a limp. When you look out into the pasture, you are not looking at perfect animals. You are looking at the ones who needed Noah's Ark.

Then there are the exotic animals, who draw over one hundred thousand visitors annually to Noah's Ark, which is open to the public year-round. Thousands of children visit the Ark for educational field trips.

"What kind of animals will I see when I come to Noah's Ark?" a caller asks the office staff. "We have over one hundred species of animals," is the answer. "You'll see ostriches, emus, peacocks, llamas, tigers, a leopard, baboons, monkeys, wolves, bears, and our 'BLT'—a lion, tiger and bear who live together as a family." The total number of animal inhabitants is now more than fifteen hundred.

Some of the animals have claimed national and even international attention. The first to make news was a white billy goat named Snowball. He had been abused by the elderly man who owned him. One day Snowball defended himself and butted the man, knocking him from the porch. The man died and authorities planned to euthanize Snowball. The public raised such an uproar about killing an animal that was simply defending itself that the authorities decided to send him to Noah's Ark instead. Upon arrival at the Ark, Snowball was neutered and put out to pasture, where he lived a long and peaceful life.

Other animals have had small claims to fame, but none caught the hearts and minds of people around the world like Evidence the zebra. On April 8, 2008, the office received a call asking if Noah's Ark would take a wounded baby zebra that had been found at a nearby exit on Interstate 75.

Jama, her oldest son, Charlie, and Allison (her soon to be daughter-in-law) headed down I-75 in the van from the children's care home to investigate. Noah's Ark didn't own a usable horse trailer at the time, and they really were not expecting the animal to be a zebra. But it was—

a little guy, about two or three months old, wearing a blue halter and a lead rope. It was soon evident that he had sustained horrendous injuries. The foal had apparently fallen out of a truck and had been struck by another vehicle. The Department of Natural Resources and law enforcement officers discussed the zebra and determined that because he had been abandoned, the site was a crime scene. "We need to take pictures; he's evidence," they said more than once. *Evidence.* "Yes, that's just what he is: evidence of God's love and of what Noah's Ark is all about." The moniker stuck and the little zebra was named.

Evidence was gathered up and taken to Noah's Ark. Dr. Karen Thomas, board member and longtime volunteer veterinarian at Noah's Ark, began triage on the zebra—the first she had ever treated. She soon realized his wounds were life-threatening.

Evidence was quickly loaded into the van and driven to the University of Auburn's College of Veterinary Science in Alabama, where tests showed that he had a shattered pelvis and a severed urethra. Jama faced Dr. Justin Harper, an equine veterinary expert, and asked, "Does he have a chance to survive?" Dr. Harper answered that he did have a chance, but not a good one.

Friends of Noah's Ark responded to a plea to save the little zebra, and Evidence received life-saving surgeries. In May 2008, he came to live at the Ark as his forever home. He wowed guests for three years until his death, in November 2010, from complications stemming from his injuries.

When word was released that Evidence the zebra had died, phone calls, emails, and letters poured into Noah's Ark from all over the nation, and even from overseas, sharing how his story had touched countless lives. People emailed to say they were weeping at the death of this brave survivor, whom they had hoped to meet someday when their travels brought them to the Atlanta area. His story of survival and acceptance had struck a chord in the hearts of many people.

The most unusual animal family at Noah's Ark is its "BLT." Baloo the American black bear, Leo the African lion, and Shere Khan the tiger came to live at Noah's Ark in 2001. These animals ranged in age from four to six months and had been confiscated during an Atlanta drug bust. When the Department of Natural Resources brought them to Noah's Ark, these three little boys had already bonded as a family.

In 2009, Noah's Ark finally received enough funding to move the unusual trio to the public habitat. Calls began to come in from the *Today Show*, *Good Morning America*, the Associated Press, Brazilian and Korean news agencies, and *National Geographic*. Baloo, Leo, and Shere Khan became household names as people all over the world began to see their story on *Unlikely Animal Friends* 2 on the National Geographic channel and Web site. In addition, they have been featured in books and calendars. This trio is a perfect example of living in harmony. They are all different from each other, yet they do not let those differences get in the way of their friendship. Their story is certainly a prelude to the Peaceable Kingdom.

Some animals come to Noah's Ark simply needing a home. Others need some medical care. Then there are those who need around-the-clock care in order to survive. It is one thing when that animal is a tiny bunny or even a lemur. It is another thing altogether when it is a big cat like Zuri the white tiger.

Zuri is a white Bengal tiger who faces many of the health concerns most inbred animals do. White tigers are not natural; their coloring is actually an inbred deformity. They suffer from a host of genetic problems and weak immune systems. Approximately one out of one hundred white tigers survive. The rest die or are euthanized due to severe deformities.

Although Zuri appears to be normal, she has an incredibly weak immune system and was near death when she came to live at Noah's Ark. Upon coming to Noah's Ark, Zuri was put into quarantine and tested to determine the cause of her hair and weight loss. Finally, after a year of treatments and tender loving care, Zuri has regrown her hair and has added one hundred much-needed pounds to her frame. At the time of this writing, Zuri is healthy enough to join the rest of the animals in the Ark's habitats, but she is awaiting a habitat of her own because of her poor genetics and low immune system. Her habitat will have an educational component to it, which will help the public understand why tigers should not be kept as pets or circus acts, and why the inbreeding of white tigers is inhumane.

Throughout the years, Noah's Ark has had its struggles. But as Jama reminds anyone who asks, the dream belongs to God, not to her. And she emphasizes that because it is God's dream, God will take care of it. There are times when the coffers are all but empty. Prayers go up, and the need is filled. And the dream does not stagnate, but continues to grow. There will always be a Caleb or Jennifer—or an Evidence or Zuri—who needs a forever home. And as long as God wishes it, there will always be a Noah's Ark waiting with open arms and open hearts, perpetuating the Peaceable Kingdom.

7

Won't Technology Save Us?
Taking Leadership on Environmental Concerns

Arthur Paul Boers

An old tale recounts a flood that forces a pious person to climb onto his roof. Convinced that God will preserve him, he refuses a ride when a friend floats by on a makeshift raft: "No worries. God will help me." He gives the same response to a stranger with an outboard motor. A police helicopter flies over, offering assistance. Again the Christian declines. The flood rises and he drowns. In heaven, he confronts God: "I thought you would save me." God responds, "I tried. I sent a friend on a raft, a stranger in a boat, and police in a helicopter."

This joke illustrates both blindness to danger *and* unwillingness to make necessary changes—much as many people these days dismiss dealing with monumental environmental problems, convinced that somehow technology will help us. Increasing numbers of scientists warn of the destructive consequences of fuel consumption, but there is not much North American consensus or willingness to make major lifestyle changes. Many believe that technological innovation and human ingenuity will solve environmental hazards. People are optimistic that all can be redressed by technology: no matter what dangers we face, no matter how serious. But political scientist Thomas Homer-Dixon reminds us that our ability to overcome problems is not clear.

> Our species' scientific and technological prowess is . . . extraordinary. We create miracles from raw nature, and we have revolutionized our existence in a few lifetimes. These accomplishments are to be celebrated. Unfortunately, they have also made us overconfident of our ability to solve the problems we face. Today, a disturbingly large proportion of people in rich countries seem to believe that our ingenuity is practically boundless and that our technical experts have all the authority and knowledge they need to deftly manage our ever more complex world. These beliefs and the complacency they produce are often completely unwarranted: in fact, we often have only superficial control over the complex systems we've made and critically depend upon.[1]

Some suggested solutions to combat climate change are spectacularly peculiar. As Bill McKibben reports, one scientist proposed "a 'fleet of several hundred jumbo jets' to ferry 35 million tons of sulfur dioxide into the stratosphere annually to reflect sunlight away from the earth" (which "would increase acid rain 'and give the blue sky a whitish cast'").[2] Alas, most technological proposals are aimed at allowing us to continue living in the profligate ways to which we've grown accustomed.

Jared Diamond also cautions against trusting in technology. We cannot be certain "that, from tomorrow onwards, technology will function primarily to solve existing problems and will cease to create new problems." Nor can we "assume that the new technologies . . . will succeed, and . . . quickly enough to make a big difference soon." Some innovations may work and others may not. Successful ones might take decades to be effective. Furthermore, consider this: "Technological solutions to environmental problems are routinely far more expensive than preventive measures to avoid creating the problem in the first place: for example, the billions of dollars of damages and cleanup costs associated

1. Homer-Dixon, *Ingenuity Gap*, 5–6.
2. McKibben, *End of Nature*, 68.

with major oil spills, compared to the modest cost of safety measures effective at minimizing the risk of a major oil spill." Perhaps most seriously: "rapid advances in technology during the twentieth century have been creating difficult new problems faster than they have been solving old problems."[3]

I would love to see technological optimism pay off, but Christians should not quietly settle for that possibility. First, technological effects and disasters have global ramifications. Second, technological innovations often have disastrously unexpected consequences, the very opposite of their intentions. Third, mature thinking requires moving beyond technical solutions to acknowledging that *we* need to change values, practices, and lifestyles.

Risking It All—Global Dangers

The stakes are high. Technology has grown hazardous—complex, intertwined, and developing rapidly. Once, mistakes affected a localized area. However, we are no longer talking about the loss of a mountain or two, a forest here or there, a lake or river or watershed—all sad and shocking enough. Now we risk *global* harm and extinction. Dangers threaten entire species. Gambling (hardly a Christian practice) is one thing, but putting everything up for grabs is another. We are not just buying a lottery ticket with a weekly paycheck but risking our entire mortgage in one roulette spin.

Jared Diamond writes on collapsed societies, ecologically destructive civilizations. Cultures commit "unintended ecological suicide—ecocide" by undermining their environments in one or more of eight ways: "deforestation and habitat destruction, soil problems (erosion, salinization, and soil fertility losses), water management problems, overhunting, overfishing, effects of introduced species on native species, human population growth, and increased per capita impact of people." On top of those eight perennial dangers that still threaten us, we added four others in recent decades: "human-caused climate change, buildup of toxic chemicals in the environment, energy shortages, and full hu-

---

3. Diamond, *Collapse*, 504, 505.

man utilization of the Earth's photosynthetic capacity."[4] Previous collapses—Easter Island, Anasazi, Pitcairn and Henderson Islands, Maya civilizations, the Vikings in Iceland and Greenland—were confined to particular geographical regions, but the threats now are global.

Environmental issues have been on the radar screen of public consciousness for decades. Yet recent concerns did not anticipate current challenges. Previously, "we spoiled and polluted parts of . . . nature" and "inflicted environmental 'damage.' But that was like stabbing a man with toothpicks: though it hurt, annoyed, degraded, it did not touch vital organs, block the path of the lymph or blood."[5] But it is now possible for technology to devastate the entire globe and atmosphere, whether by nuclear war, nuclear accidents, or other technological effects, including acid rain, "ozone depletion, global warming, ecosystem destruction, the population explosion, polluted land, air, streams, and oceans, and human and mechanical errors."[6] Such doomsday possibilities were once inconceivable, except to fevered and fantastic apocalyptic imaginations.

We have altered everything, even the weather, as Bill McKibben, an early voice warning of global warming, observes: "We have changed the atmosphere, and thus we are changing the weather. By changing the weather, we make every spot on earth man-made and artificial. We have deprived nature of its independence, and that is fatal to its meaning."[7] Or consider that "we each consume suspected carcinogens released into the environment by people far removed from us in space and time. Some of the chemical contaminants we carry in our bodies are pesticides sprayed by farmers we have never met, whose language we may not speak, in countries whose agricultural practices may be completely unfamiliar to us."[8] And we have our reliance on technology to thank. All of the ecological hazards and challenges we face are a result of how we use technology. Not all change equals progress.

While technology once helped overcome natural dangers, now nature is at risk because of technology. A natural world that previously

4. Ibid., 3, 6, 7, 135.
5. McKibben, *End of Nature*, 48.
6. Strong, *Crazy Mountains*, 79.
7. McKibben, *End of Nature*, 58.
8. Steingraber, *Living Downstream*, 179.

threatened us is now threatened by us. The unprecedented hazards suggest that what Martin Luther King Jr. eloquently articulated decades ago holds true, now more than ever: "We have allowed our technology to outrun our theology." As Thoreau writes in *Walden*, "our inventions . . . are but improved means to an unimproved end."[9] Political scientist Thomas Homer-Dixon warns, "When we look back from the year 2100, I fear we will see a period when our creations--technological, social, and ecological—outstripped our understanding and we lost control of our destiny."[10]

Technology Bites Back—Unintended Consequences and Revenge Effects

Innovations often exacerbate the very problems they allegedly address. Then we respond with further technological innovations. Cars were invented to address transportation needs, but our cities were then reshaped to accommodate cars. Many cities now deal with the debilitating effects of traffic jams and commuter congestion. With more highways, people commute farther. With energy efficient cars we drive longer distances and generate more pollution.

Edward Tenner observes how technology improves much in our lives yet has many "revenge effects." He is not speaking of accidents. One might remember Chernobyl (the true costs of which—in terms of lost lives, injuries, geographical devastation, and subsequent illnesses— were never accurately tallied). Or the Deepwater Horizon oil spill. Or the gas leak at the Union Carbide pesticide plant in Bhopal, India, which resulted in approximately four thousand deaths and two hundred thousand injuries.[11] Wendell Berry is scathing about such incidents: "How would you describe the difference between modern war and modern industry—between, say, bombing and strip mining, or between chemical warfare and chemical manufacturing? The difference seems to be

9. Thoreau, *Walden*, 1:84.

10. Homer-Dixon, *Ingenuity Gap*, 8.

11. Diamond, *Collapse*, 446. A lengthy list of other toxic consequences of technology, affecting millions of people, can be found in Glendinning, *When Technology Wounds*, 18–20.

only that in war the victimization of humans is directly intentional and in industry it is 'accepted' as a 'trade-off.' Were the catastrophes of Love Canal, Bhopal, Chernobyl, and the *Exxon Valdez* episodes of war or of peace? They were, in fact, peacetime acts of aggression, intentional to the extent that risks were known and ignored."[12]

Such eventualities are no small price to pay for progress, but are not "revenge effects." Nor does Tenner mean simply side effects or unfortunate by-products. Revenge effects are consequences that are the opposite of a technology's intended purpose. "If a cancer chemotherapy treatment causes baldness, that is not a revenge effect, but if it induces another, equally lethal cancer, that is a revenge effect."[13] The cure's cost is as serious and harmful as the illness being treated. A "revenge effect" is no mere trade-off.

Technology sometimes accomplishes the opposite of what it promises: "In Philadelphia, only 3,000 of 157,000 calls from automatic security systems over three years were real; by diverting the full-time equivalent of fifty-eight police officers for useless calls, the systems may have promoted crimes elsewhere."[14] National Park Service rangers receive more and more calls from hikers with cellular phones; as Barbara Brown Taylor notes, "Very few are genuine emergencies. The majority are from people who have gotten lost and want to be guided back to their cars by phone, or who have developed painful blisters on their feet and want someone to come pick them up."[15]

Not only does such behavior tax and divert public services, but technological devices move people away from necessary wilderness etiquette and skills. Technology, supposed to make us safer, actually led to inadequately prepared wayfarers and caused increased hazards for rangers. Trusting a technological solution often leads to risky behavior.

Not long ago futurists predicted that with digital technology, our offices, lives, and institutions would become "paperless." In fact, we use

12. Berry, *What Are People For?*, 202.
13. Tenner, *Why Things Bite Back*, 8.
14. Ibid., 8–9. See also 294.
15. Taylor, *When God Is Silent*, 444. See also Tenner, *Why Things Bite Back*, 294–95.

more paper than ever: "Globally, paper consumption increased more than sixfold over the latter half of the twentieth century."[16]

Or consider these examples:

- Rising reliance on air-conditioning ups outdoor temperatures in cities.[17]

- Improved "overall health" amplifies the significance of chronic illness: "Sometimes longer life has meant a sicker life."[18]

- As surgery hurts less, people have more operations and have "possibly increased the sum of medically induced pain, especially postoperatively."[19]

- Major industrial measures taken to address air pollution contributed to acid rain.[20]

- Improved running shoes make it possible to run farther and easier, "multiplying stresses to joints, tendons, muscles, and bones."[21]

- Because of safety devices, people more confidently engage in extreme and risky sports.[22]

- "Massive shielding of beaches from the energy of waves has deflected their intensity to other shores or robbed these beaches of replenishing sand."[23]

- Successful forest fire fighting "helped build reservoirs of flammable materials in the understory for more intense [fires]."[24]

- "Rigid molded ski boots . . . helped prevent ankle and tibia fractures at the cost of anterior cruciate ligament injuries."[25]

16. Worldwatch Institute, *State of the World 2004*, 142.
17. Tenner, *Why Things Bite Back*, 9.
18. Ibid., 34–35. See also 62.
19. Ibid., 42.
20. Ibid., 109.
21. Ibid., 281.
22. Ibid., 294–95.
23. Ibid., 325.
24. Ibid.
25. Ibid.

- Because of the increasing use of antibiotics not just to cure ill-ness but to prevent it both in humans and livestock, "bacteria have evolved ways of defending themselves. Today, as a result, we're facing a crisis of antibiotic resistance in bacterial species ranging from common strains of salmonella to the often lethal *Staphylococcus aureus* and *Mycobacterium tuberculosis*."[26]

- Catalytic converters in cars were designed "to reduce urban smog . . . but . . . turn out to be a major source of nitrous oxide, a powerful greenhouse gas."[27]

- "Efforts in the U.S. to eradicate the ferocious fire ant using an arsenal of pesticides wiped out its parasites and competing spe-cies of ant; there followed an explosion of the fire ant population across hundreds of millions of hectares of the U.S. South and Southwest."[28]

- The staggering increase in information technologies seemed to promise greater insight. Now an average individual "spends ever more time on basic tasks of managing information, and ever less time producing creative ideas and truly useful knowledge."[29]

- "Sales of antibacterial soap, tooth whiteners and 'intimate hy-giene' products (wipes and sprays) are skyrocketing. Scientists actually connect the rising rates of asthma and allergies in the West to our overzealous cleanliness."[30]

- Weed killers result in secondary pests.[31]

- "Unemployment has risen each decade of the information age, with the increasing deployment of 'labour-saving' technology."[32]

In the above examples, technology made situations worse. These are not occasional, random, or trivial instances. We have no idea what

26. Homer-Dixon, *Ingenuity Gap*, 175.
27. Ibid., 178.
28. Ibid.
29. Ibid., 209.
30. Ashenburg, "Our Enemy Hands."
31. Steingraber, *Living Downstream*, 154.
32. Noble, *Progress Without People*, xii.

effects could be sparked by technological solutions to environmental crises. And there will be little time to correct ensuing damage, especially as technological change continues to accelerate exponentially. Relying on unspecified technological solutions could likewise lure us into behaving in even more ecologically hazardous ways. It is not enough to solve problems technologically. We must examine priorities, values, and lifestyles.

Let's Get Adaptive—Moving Beyond Technical and Technological Solutions

Ronald Heifetz explains a crucial distinction between technical and adaptive challenges: "The most common cause of failure in leadership is produced by treating adaptive challenges as if they were technical problems."[33] This distinction is revealing when pondering whether or not technology can save us from environmental woes.

Heifetz notes that during crises and uncertainty we often turn to experts for help. Or we rely on programs or technologies. No one denies that authorities, programs, and technologies have their uses and contribute much to human well-being. His point, however, is that we face many problems that no authority, expert, program, or technology can solve:

> Examples abound: poverty at home and abroad, industrial competitiveness, failing schools, drug abuse, the national debt, racial prejudice, ethnic strife, AIDS, environmental pollution. No organizational response can be called into play that will clearly resolve these kinds of problems. No clear expertise can be found, no single sage has general credibility, no established procedure will suffice.[34]

Leadership means helping people face distressing circumstances, claim their agency, and address issues. "Habitually seeking solutions from people in authority is maladaptive."[35]

33. Heifetz, Grashow, and Linsky, *Practice of Adaptive Leadership*, 19.

34. Heifetz, *Leadership without Easy Answers*, 72.

35. Ibid., 73.

Technical challenges have several characteristics:[36]

- The problem is clear.

- The solution is clear.

- The authority is clear.

Technical problems are satisfying for the afflicted and the expert as well. As a boy I accidentally sliced open my thumb while playing on the beach. I had a technical challenge:

- The problem was a wound that needed tending.

- The solution was to clean it and have it stitched.

- The expert who solved my problem was the emergency room doctor.

Adaptive problems are different:

- Defining the problem itself is not clear and requires learning.

- Resolving the problem involves "changes in . . . priorities, beliefs, habits, and loyalties."[37]

- The one responsible for addressing the issue is not necessarily an external authority.

When I once struggled with burnout, I had an adaptive problem:

- I did not know whether this was a matter of overwork, emotional weakness, ingrained family patterns, or a temporary matter that might resolve itself. I did not know what would help. This burnout was a call to increased self-awareness.

- I went for counseling to recover equanimity and learn new ways of functioning.

- No one could do this for me. A counselor worked with me, but I was the one who had to learn new priorities, values, and behaviors.

Many challenges combine the technical and adaptive. When my father had a heart attack, coronary health was the obvious concern. The solutions mixed technical (medication, naps, vacations) and adap-

---

36. Heifetz shows all of this in a chart in ibid., 76.

37. Heifetz, Grashow, and Linsky, *Practice of Adaptive Leadership*, 19.

tive (coping with stress, slowing down, decreasing his cigarette use). Physicians helped with technical matters (treatment, prescriptions), but the onus was on my father to learn new behaviors. Dealing with adaptive and adaptive-technical challenges is hard and demanding work. Not surprisingly, many shy away. "Indeed," writes Heifetz, "the harsher the reality, the harder we look to an authority for a remedy that saves us from adjustment. By and large, we want answers, not questions. Even the toughest individual tends to avoid realities that require adaptive work, searching instead for an authority to provide the way out."[38]

In 1979, Jimmy Carter gave what became known as his "malaise" speech. He told the nation that it had to reduce dependence on foreign oil. He suggested less consumption, fewer car trips, lowered thermostats, and driving slower. While the suggestions were practical and appear technical, he was calling for a lifestyle change—asking Americans to learn new habits and values. Carter's speech went over badly.[39] Many people were unwilling to change how they lived.

No one has the know-how or expertise to solve global climate change. To slow it—let alone turn it around—will take massive efforts and major lifestyle shifts. Adaptive challenges "call for changes of heart and mind—the transformation of long-standing habits and deeply held assumptions and values."[40] Author James Howard Kunstler found resistance when he traveled across America and explained the implications of peak oil concerns. Kunstler recalls that people asked for "solutions": "They were clamoring desperately for rescue remedies that would allow them to continue living exactly the way they were used to living, with all the accustomed comforts ranging from endless driving to universal air-conditioning, cheap fast food, reliable electric service, NASCAR, Disney World, Walmart, and *good jobs* with a guaranteed comfortable retirement. They didn't want to hear anything that suggested we might have to make other arrangements for everyday life in this country." Such "solutions" merely look "for ways to sustain the unsustainable."[41]

38. Heifetz, *Leadership without Easy Answers*, 76.
39. Ibid., 180.
40. Parks, *Leadership Can Be Taught*, 10.
41. Kunstler, *Too Much Magic*, 7.

Not all civilizations avert catastrophe. With no prior experience of such issues, they may not appreciate the gravity of their situation. (Human-influenced global climate change is certainly unprecedented.) Or drawing a false analogy, they assume that prior solutions will work, trying to apply previously successful techniques to contemporary adaptive quandaries. Other reasons for failing to deal adequately with a problem include not realizing an issue's gravity, especially as it assumes a "creeping normalcy" (like the proverbial frog in slowly heating water). Many societies do not respond even to challenges they know to be real—whether because of selfishness, short-term goals, or other pitfalls. Once people recognize the issue, "the problem may be beyond our present capacities to solve, a solution may be prohibitively expensive, our efforts may be too little and too late."[42] This may now be the case for us and climate change.

Conclusion

Rather than despairingly hoping for messianic scientific advances and technological delivery, we need to be intentional about choosing different directions.

We must not rely on technology to escape our ecological morass. We have to learn new ways of living. Many resist such developments, but I welcome them. Even if global climate change is not a hazard, we have much to gain from changing habits. Kunstler believes we will soon rely less on cars. Farming will become relocalized; more people will regain the ability to grow and store food. People will produce their own entertainment: "we're going to have to make our own music and our own drama. . . . We're going to need playhouses and live performance halls. We're going to need violin and banjo players and playwrights and scenery-makers, and singers."[43]

Schools will be decentralized. "Life . . . will . . . become more local, and virtually all the activities of everyday life will . . . be re-scaled." Changes will be challenging, but many will immeasurably benefit us. As a result of our decreased reliance on fossil fuel, we may have cleaner air

42. Diamond, *Collapse*, 421, 423, 425.
43. Kuntler, "Ten Ways to Prepare for a Post-Oil Society."

and water, grow up healthier, reduce smog, and rely more on walking and cycling. Such adaptive changes, which Kunstler calls "intelligent responses," "are likely to put us back in touch with elements of human experience that we thoughtlessly discarded in our heedless rush toward a techno-nirvana—working together with people we know, spending time with friends and loved ones, sharing food with people we love, and enacting the other ceremonies of daily and seasonal life in story and song."[44] That all sounds promisingly attractive.

Advanced technology is not necessarily going to save us, and we may not actually want it to do so. And there is no reason to expect God to get us out of our morass, either. But we still have the capacity to choose to live into a much more promising future. I call that the good life.

44. Kunstler, *Too Much Magic*, 7–8.

8

Aren't Humans Stewards of God's Creation? On the Moral Importance of Naming Ourselves in Relation to the Land

Kelly Johnson

FOR MANY YEARS, SCHOLARS, teachers, and preachers have relied on stewardship language to encourage people to care more for the earth. The argument runs something like this: Because humans are stewards of the earth rather than its owners, they must care for the earth according to God's laws and in ways that will allow others' lives to flourish— whether those others are nonhuman animals or humans. People have made many noble attempts at conservation and other efforts to help life thrive on earth under the rubric of stewardship. I will argue, however, that stewardship was not a good approach to begin with, and at any rate, it has failed. The question before us is no longer, "How should we care for the earth?" but "How will we live with the damage we have caused and continue to cause?"

What's Wrong with Stewardship?

The English term *stewardship* has such theological resonance that theologian Douglas John Hall notes that even German theologians have occasionally adopted the word without translating it. The fact that the term *stewardship* has such significance suggests that its full import is tied to the historical English-speaking contexts in which it emerged as a moral category.[1] Who has used it and to do what kinds of work? How did it become popular?

Prior to the Reformation, *stewardship* appeared occasionally in English theological work to refer to God (who distributes all good). In the sixteenth century, writers began using the word principally to describe human action, especially Christian control of power and wealth. Right around the same time, the English crown seized the wealth of all monasteries in its territory and redistributed much of it to favored laypeople. Those entrusted with this property, so the logic ran, served God by rescuing the church from the temptations of wealth. Edward Sandys, preaching some forty years later in Elizabeth I's court, urged those who had profited from that process to be "stewards" of the blessings of wealth that God had entrusted to them. He did not reflect on the fact that the King—not God—had actually been the giver.

So stewardship named a moral office that the holders of God-given private property inhabited. While God is the source of the authority, the steward, acting in God's place, fills in the specifics of what to do and how to do it.

This line of thought is so familiar to us now that it may be difficult to hear anything remarkable in it. Notice, though, that early proponents of stewardship saw it as closely related to the Christian practice of holy poverty. These stewards carried the burden of managing wealth so that the clergy and religious could properly fulfill their calling to poverty. Stewards of wealth justified their position as a way of participating in the exemplary lives of those who renounced personal wealth and power. But stewardship of wealth quickly displaced voluntary poverty as a central moral practice. While otherworldly saints might be poor and holy, those servants of God who actually cared for the poor and promoted earthly progress were useful and productive. The great nineteenth-century missionary expansions taught Western Christians to see themselves as stewards responsible for bringing the gospel—as well as hygiene and capitalism—to the passive, impoverished, pagan masses of

1. I make this argument in greater detail in Johnson, *The Fear of Beggars*.

the world. Ownership and efficient use, rather than humble poverty and patient hope in God, become hallmarks of Christian excellence.

Given this history, the term *stewardship* has come to signify pragmatic, lay-centered, efficiency-oriented Christian responsibility for the world, authorized by God and serving ends broadly associated with God's purposes for the world, as the individual owner interprets them. In most cases, discussions of stewardship skip over any question of whether wealth is justly gained. All private property is presumed to be given by God. Moral discernment about how to use wealth and power is between an individual and God, with little to no role for communal responsibility or church authority. The spirit of stewardship is paternalistic, depicting the holder of wealth and power as God's agent for the sake of those less gifted. For good or ill, these layers of meaning are now part of talk about stewardship.

But Isn't Environmental Stewardship Different?

Perhaps, however, environmental stewardship evades many of the problems that plagued economic stewardship. Arising as it does with environmental consciousness, it has a concern not only for private property but particularly for what is common—the sea, air, climate. There is strong scriptural warrant for calling creation God's blessing for the benefit of all and no danger that the "blessing'" of creation should instead be described as ill-gotten gains. Environmental stewardship concerns all people, regardless of race or class, and advocates of environmental stewardship often hold up as heroes not the ruling class but Native Americans and other indigenous groups previously held in low regard. Environmental stewardship, then, is less prone than economic stewardship to paper over injustice and selfishness, more likely to build on communal concerns and judgments, and far more likely to be free of class and race paternalism.

Right?

Richard Bauckham has pointed out that even in the context of ecology, stewardship is a problematic moral category.[2] Environmental stewardship, like its financial predecessor, demands responsibility but

2. Bauckham, *Bible and Ecology*, 1–36.

does little to fill in the details of what that responsibility must look like. Summarizing the work of many scholars, Bauckham points out that appeals to stewardship are perniciously vague. Judgments about what courses we should follow depend on what goods we think we ought to promote and how we think we can and should act. On such details, environmental stewardship has little to say. Is stewardship about managing resources efficiently to meet human needs, or does it require attention to the good of other creatures in their own right?[3] Are all means equally valuable for reaching our goals, or are there goods internal to certain methods? In environmental stewardship, as in financial stewardship, the steward has enormous leeway to define what "stewardship" requires.

For example, the Environmental Stewardship Program, sponsored by Dow Agrosciences, the National Cattlemen's Beef Association, the National Resources Conservation Service, and the U.S. Fish and Wildlife Service, gives an annual award to U.S. cattle producers who "desire to leave the land in better shape for future generations." That description sits somewhat uneasily with the claim, found on the program's Web site, that "the environment and conserving natural resources are of high importance to cattlemen and women, *because these resources directly affect their bottom-line.*"[4] Concern for the bottom-line in the U.S. economy is notoriously susceptible to short-term pressures. At any rate, while it makes sense that those who raise cattle should be supported when they resist such short-term pressures regarding the use of water and pastureland, questions about how cattle will be raised, fed, maintained, and killed will be more difficult to consider in this forum. So will larger questions about the economics of a meat-centered diet in a world of expanding population. As in economic stewardship, general appeals to responsibility leave a wide swath of moral ground to be cleared.

Similarly, while it is true that Scripture names creation as a blessing given by God, talk about environmental stewardship suffers from

---

3. Benedict XVI has attempted to describe stewardship (English translation for dominion) in such a way that humans use creation but also recognize that it is not merely material for human use. Nature, he says, is "more than raw material to be manipulated at our pleasure; it is a wondrous work of the Creator containing a 'grammar' which sets forth ends and criteria for its wise use, not its reckless exploitation." Pope Benedict XVI, *Caritas in Veritate*, 99–101 (§48).

4. For these statements, see www.environmentalstewardship.org.

the same silence as financial stewardship when it comes to the history of ownership. We saw that in economic stewardship, naming possessions "blessings" allowed us to forget the histories that have produced our current patterns of ownership. In the case of environmental steward-ship, the same pernicious forgetfulness applies. Why are certain people given charge of certain lands, creatures, ecosystems? Do histories of conquest and patterns of distribution of wealth have anything to do with "stewardship"?

But the deepest problem Bauckham explores is that appeals to stewardship depict God as absent and passive: it is we humans who must act in God's place. We are therefore less a part of a creation governed by God than we are beings above creation, acting in God's stead. Such a claim depends on and promotes a kind of hubris, a false confidence that humans can and should control all creation. This understanding of stewardship is typically rooted in an interpretation of an isolated though important scriptural text, Genesis 1:26–28, in which God says of humans, "let them have dominion over the fish of the sea, and over the birds of the air, and over the cattle, and over all the earth, and over every creeping thing that creeps upon the earth," and commands hu-mans to "fill the earth and subdue it; and have dominion over the fish of the sea and over the birds of the air and over every living thing that moves upon the earth."

Much hangs on our understanding of what it means for humans to "have dominion" and to "subdue the earth." What can be said briefly here is that nothing in the text indicates that God will be absent or that nonhuman creation is dangerously out of control without human man-agement. God does not authorize humans to ignore the purposes given to other creatures on each of the days God declares "good," nor does God tell humans to fix a wild and dangerous disorder. Rather, God gives humans their place in the land they should settle and cultivate; God gives humans a particular role, a share in God's dominion, which is not mere instrumental use, but a kind of care that allows a wide variety of lives to flourish together. Humans are members of God's creation, which the first creation story repeatedly declares to be good even before humans appear on the scene.

Because stewardship pictures that ultimate authority, God, as absent, it instills in owners a sense of "responsibility" that is in tension with the virtues of patience and humility. Humans must act in place of God, managing a complex world of limited goods. Small wonder, then, that both financial and environmental stewardship alike have been associated with efficient maximization of productivity for human ends.

Stewardship talk is rife with opportunities for self-deception, confusing hubris with tragic responsibility for a world in which God is absent. As stewards of the earth, people may feel authorized or even required to use nonhuman creation in shortsighted or merely instrumentalist ways, without attending to the interdependence of human and nonhuman life and without respecting the goodness and beauty of creation in its own right.

But it is also true that as stewards of the earth, people may feel burdened with an impossible load, responsible to care for more creatures than we even know exist, accountable for our impact on systems we still do not entirely understand, charged to oversee all that is and bring it to its fulfillment, though we are not even clear on what our own fulfillment will be exactly. Conscientious Christians worry that if we fail to make it all turn out right, to use creation in ever more profitable ways, we will be judged harshly. Stewardship fails, both practically and spiritually, to set us in right relationship with God and creation.

So What Now?

Evidence of the failure of stewardship as moral language can be found in the widespread and catastrophic environmental abuse that has occurred during its tenure. While individual weather events cannot be equated with or simply blamed on climate change, the trends of the past twenty-five years are clear.[5] Sea levels have risen. Heat waves and droughts have increased in frequency and intensity. Weather patterns are shifting, and growing seasons are changing. As a result, food supplies have become less certain, water rights more contentious, poverty more dangerous.

5. A carefully researched and readable summary of current findings is available in Climate Central, *Global Weirdness*. See 116–19 for a discussion of specific extreme weather events in relation to longer-term trends.

Particular trouble awaits those who have fewer resources, fewer options, and less flexibility as they face rising seas, intense storms, drought and flood, damaged harvests, and lost species. All humans are in peril, but as usual, it will be people mired in poverty who will face the worst consequences. Moreover, the rest of God's creation—nonhuman animals, plants, the whole living system of the planet—are already suffering grave harm, and signs are that they are headed for worse. We will be living (and in fact already are living) in a world that we have damaged, perhaps irreparably, with grave effects on all of God's good creation.

If ever we believed that we were authorized and competent to be in charge of creation on God's behalf, if ever stewardship were a good image for reflection on the role of humans in creation, that moment is over. We still have to live in creation among other creatures, thus using resources, and we should try to discover better ways to do that. But the illusion that we are wise caretakers who know what is best for all has been destroyed. Now we must act in the knowledge that we have created harm. We have damaged the earth and each other, for now and for the future. Our proper role now is as penitents.[6]

What are penitents? First, penitents are those who recognize their guilt. Historically, Christians have given abundant advice on examining our consciences regarding our relationships to other persons and to God, but we have relatively little practice at examining our consciences regarding our relations to nonhuman creation. Nevertheless, the faults—pride, sloth, greed, and envy, for starters—are no strangers to us. In what thoughts, words, and deeds, committed and omitted, have we placed ourselves above rather than within creation? Have we noted and respected the goodness God creates in every being, or have we treated creatures—human and nonhuman—as instruments to satisfy

6. This has been a particular theme of the Patriarch Bartholomew of Constantinople, who, in his 2003 "Message for the Day of the Protection of the Environment," wrote that our prayer to be forgiven as we forgive others "should be accompanied by a corresponding sacrifice, mainly a sacrifice of our selfishness and arrogant pursuits, which demonstrate our insolent attitude towards the Creator and His wisely stipulated natural and spiritual laws. This change of attitude and mentality is called repentance. Only if our prayer to God for the protection of the environment is accompanied by correspondent repentance, will it be effective and welcomed by God" (Patriarch Bartholomew of Constantinople, "Message," par. 4).

our own purposes? Have we discerned our true happiness as members of creation, or have we aimed to secure for ourselves a "happiness" that we can claim and control alone? Such an examination of conscience will have to consider our individual and collective responsibilities.

Genuine recognition of guilt is a psychologically and morally complex process. A common first response among those who on some level recognize guilt is to deny it and to deny doing any harm—to avoid looking at it, to "move forward" by refusing to see that anything has in fact changed. If we cannot deny the grave and lasting harm, then we may try at least to minimize our responsibility for it. We create excuses, some of which we may even believe. We deceive ourselves into believing that our own role was innocent or at least insignificant.

Such self-deception becomes even more powerful when a whole society engages in it together to sustain not only their individual sense of self but also to sustain a social order. A 2011 study tells of a community in Norway where people agreed that climate change is real and is caused by human activity and where they often commented on the change in their own climate—the lack of snow for skiing—and the impact on their economy and culture.[7] In this community, people were well informed about political issues and had high levels of civic engagement. In spite of recognizing the role of human activity in climate change, they did nothing to change their own behaviors or to pressure local companies and the national government to change behaviors. They strove instead to create a sense of stability and normalcy, to deny that Norway (an oil-exporting country) had any significant responsibility or power.

The collective refusal of most societies to address climate change seems based in the fear that any admission of guilt will irrevocably damage our sense of who we are and the stability of our world. We cannot bear to face the truth of what we have done. We cannot imagine living on the other side of that guilt.

Guilt can be a trap, of course. But true penitents do not have the luxury of despair. They have to face each day anew, making amends when possible and learning to live in the truth. The life of Christian penance is not about settling into self-hatred. In fact, the joyful Francis of Assisi described his vocation as a life of penance.

7. Norgaard, *Living in Denial*.

The story of Zaccheus (Luke 19:1–10) provides a particularly rich model of how penitence opens out into life. As the story opens, the tax collector seems unrepentant about his abuse of power. Perhaps he convinced himself that he filled a necessary role, that he had not created the financial system of the Roman Empire but only navigated it in a sensible way. He may have thought of God as absent, leaving humans to muddle along on their own. Someone, after all, had to keep the Romans satisfied so that they would not crush the population. Perhaps he told himself that he acted responsibly, for the sake of all, making use of the burden of power he had been given.

It is important to the story that Zaccheus is short. He uses his position to be powerful in a world where people like him were unlikely to be in power. But his authority is fragile. Such a man would want to see the famous Jesus as he passes through Jericho. Zaccheus is drawn to power like a moth to a candle, and Jesus has power over crowds as well as demons. But Zaccheus does not ask people to make room for him. He climbs a tree so that he can command a view on his own terms. The small man sets himself above the crowd.

Jesus sees Zaccheus. This is the dangerous moment of truth, the unmasking of pretense, the call to penance. Here is what that sounds like: Jesus informs Zaccheus that he must come down and be the host. At Jesus's word, Zaccheus leaves his high place, comes down among the people, and repents of his fraud. As Mary prophesied, the mighty one— or in this case, a small person puffing himself up to appear mighty—has been cast down, and the lowly lifted up (Luke 1:51–52). But being cast down is not the end of his life or creativity. It is, rather, the invitation to recognize himself as a member of the community.

The miracle in Zaccheus is that Jesus overcomes that fear of facing the truth. He does not confront or accuse the little man who has put himself above others. Rather, Jesus gives him a new role. The old identity, as steward for the Roman Empire, is superseded. Now he will be host for a wandering preacher and his raggedy band of associates. The poor sort of security that Zaccheus's tax-collecting offered, so fragile that falsehoods and rationalization had to buttress it on all sides, can surrender to a new confidence. Jesus "casts down the mighty from their thrones and lifts up the lowly," and it turns out to be the best thing that ever happened to Zaccheus.

For many of us, the most difficult part of Christian teaching about repentance may be accepting forgiveness. This, along with recognizing guilt and committing to change, is a traditional component of penitence. Forgiveness does not mean that we get off the hook. Accepting such forgiveness means living with terrible truths, and living past them. We are not innocent. The harm we have done will not disappear. We must go on in a world we have damaged, in a world that is our own home, our own family. What redemption may await us we cannot know. What we can do is "come down" from our high places and open ourselves to those we have harmed. Together, we will face a future in which we are not heroes, and not even good stewards, but only creatures who repent and hope in God. With us, as with Zaccheus, the guilt of the presumptuous steward is superseded by a new, more modest and more hospitable role. That is good news.

Good news—but not easy news. The crowds saw Zaccheus's conversion as a very powerful sign, for the text says that "they supposed that the kingdom of God was to appear immediately" (Luke 19:11). We just repent and everything will start going better, right? In response, Jesus tells the Parable of the Talents, in which a tyrannical king praises two servants for making a profit out of the money entrusted to them and condemns a third for returning the full amount without increase. This, however, is no call to responsible stewardship, although the Matthean parallel is often interpreted that way. Here a tyrant with borrowed power praises servants who exploit others, and he rejects the one who behaves justly, returning to the king what is his and no more. He blames that servant for not taking usury (a practice forbidden in Scripture). In light of Zaccheus's offer to repay anyone he has defrauded, the parable is not likely to be praising government servants who know how to wring more revenue from the populace. The parable, instead, is a sobering reminder that those who do justice should not expect to have an easy road. The rejection of the honest servant foreshadows Jesus's own rejection and death.[8]

8. Myers and Debode, "Towering Trees and 'Talented Slaves.'"

We must not be naïve about the future. Telling the truth and opening up to community with the very world we have harmed is no quick fix. It is likely to bring us into conflict with those rebellious powers of the world, inside and outside ourselves, that do not rejoice in conversion. No Christian story of sin and redemption can ignore the cross.

But even the cross is good news, and even now, even in the midst of climate change. This is not the comfort of self-deception or even despair. It is the harder joy of recognizing the truth about ourselves and knowing that God does not give up on us, even then. We are not in control and we will not escape the damage we have done. Our broken and humbled hearts become the desert in which we meet that truth, and the crucified one already waits for us there. That we are invited to live in that truth is the basis for all our hope.

9

Aren't We Responsible for the Environment?

Samuel Ewell and Claudio Oliver

FROM AN ECOLOGICALLY MINDED perspective, the idea that humans are responsible for the environment is pervasive and entrenched. After all, evidence continues to mount that we are primarily responsible for climate change and other environmental catastrophes. When trying to educate others about human participation in this mess, and about how they can help alleviate it, we often ask the question, "Aren't we humans responsible for the environment?" in order to help others see their own role in both the destruction and the solution. But the more we hear about human responsibility for the environment, the more we overlook a potential blind spot. Or, to use another metaphor, responsibility can be like a mirage that tricks us into perceiving something on the horizon that is not really there. Within the "responsibility mirage," we lose the true horizon we need to move forward and confuse human *vocation* upon the earth with exercising human *control* over the planet.

The slogan "human responsibility for the environment" makes us feel empowered to solve problems. We contend, however, that this slogan can actually perpetuate the central problem of the environmental crisis, which is that human responsibility and power—not *self-limitation*—is what we need to rediscover. We can be responsible *for* or *to* something. For example, an infant's parent is responsible *for* the child, who needs the parent for touch, food, and nurture. The parent of an eighteen-year-old is responsible *to* the grown child, who no longer directly depends upon the parent for survival. Both parent-child relationships involve care and nurture, but the way of being responsible is relative to relationship's limits. Given this distinction, we can ask what kind of relationship humanity has with the environment. Does it make sense to speak of humanity as responsible *for* it or *to* it?

Biblical wisdom reminds us that the true horizon for discerning our relationship with creation is *God's relationship with all creatures of the earth*: "The earth is the Lord's and all that is in it." (Ps 24:1). Like a small child with a loving parent, all creation—including us—depends and relies upon God. Within this biblical framework, we overhear the truth which dispels the mirage and shows a true horizon: *a*) only God is responsible *for* creation, *b*) all creatures are called to give a response to God, and *c*) we get responsibility wrong by confusing our responsibility *to* God with God's responsibility *for* creation.

There is an old gospel spiritual that goes, "He's got the whole world in his hands."[1] But the dominant take on human responsibility today flips the subject: "*We've* got the whole world in *our* hands." In this tune, we no longer hear and speak the truth about ourselves and our place in the world. By contrast, the old tune tells us how we fit in God's world as caring image-bearers; how only God is responsible *for* creation; and how we—along with the whole "community of creation"—are called to be response-able *to* God. The real issue is not one of action versus passivity, but rather which human action fits with our place within creation. This raises a question: How are we called to care for creation as our human response to this God?

The Parable of the Toilet[2]

As a way of approaching the question, consider the following parable about people, place, and how (not) to be response-able.

1. We have chosen not to change the gendered language for God in this lyric in order to preserve its familiarity.
2. This parable is a revision of Claudio's original version in his book *Relationality*.

Brother Joe wanted to become a missionary to a supposedly "primitive" tribe. This tribe got their water from a river they considered sacred, and they treated their surroundings as common land, not thinking that anybody owned it individually. Their myths, celebrations, shared work, and traditions all reinforced their view of their homeland.

To prepare for missionary work to the tribe, Joe took the best classes in community development, participatory empowerment, and intercultural studies, until he finally felt prepared to go and serve the tribe. Once there, Joe decided that the tribe needed a cleaner source of water than the river. So he commissioned a short-term mission team to build an artesian well, which most people in the tribe—though not all the elders—welcomed enthusiastically because it provided abundant and clean water without much effort. The well even helped convert some people to Christianity. But the river became no more than a source of food and leisure.

Then Brother Joe decided to address sanitation in the tribe. He installed the tribe's first Western toilet, which not only flushed away the tribe's personal waste but also provided each person with privacy. Yet children who spent time swimming and playing in the river or romping around the sewage pipes started to get more parasite infestations. So Joe had a missionary team bring vaccines and worm medicine. He also started a missionary school in order to educate the tribe on health matters, and a health clinic, sponsored by a pharmaceutical company, in order to rid people of their dependence on the traditional medicine man and local remedies and provide them with cheap Western medicine.

After these advances, the local tribe became a village, as more and more people moved there. A local food supply program was launched, with new professionals arriving and some of the villagers becoming locally trained professional helpers. After thirty years of service, Joe retired and returned home. What about the river? A new missionary made plans for its cleanup and recovery.

Arriving back home, Joe noticed that the poor people around him were quite similar to those he had left behind. The problems with sewage, waste, unemployment, and violence there and in other parts of his country were very similar to those that had arisen in the tribal lands after his arrival. Then he realized that he had unwittingly reproduced these Western problems among the tribe he served for so many years.

Now Imagine a Different Story

Brother Joe met and fell in love with the tribe. Then he decided to spend more time with them on subsequent "friendship trips." Following in Jesus's footsteps, he learned about emptying himself and taking the form of the other. Listening patiently to myths and personal stories, Joe learned about the river and the tribe's relationship with it, which seemed to him a sound way of living sustainably with creation.

Aware of the problems that pollution created in his hometown, Joe investigated how the tribe had managed their human waste for so long, yet had a wonderful, clean, fertile environment. He learned about their traditional customs for dealing with feces, which required thoughtful action and sharing among the people. They showed him how to transform his own waste into manure through composting.

In time Joe learned a great many things from the tribe. For example, he learned about local plants and vegetables, including their therapeutic value and uses. He also discovered that the tribe's celebrations had similarities to his faith and shed light on his own perception of God and God's creation. He became a close friend with some elders and eventually became an elder himself. People began to respect his Christian wisdom and asked about his faith.

When he went home every year, he shared his new knowledge and insights with his parish and neighborhood and even worked with them to make their first composting toilet. This inspired the local activists to recover the ancient art of taking care of one's own waste, which became a local city initiative that included a new urban agriculture program.

Teams of parishioners began visiting Brother Joe's tribe on "friendship trips." They came as learners who wanted to discover new ways to build a sustainable life in their local setting: not emulating the tribe, but being inspired by them. Over the years, knowledge and love flowed between the two groups, and this network birthed celebrations, a deeper spirituality, and lots of learning.

Delinking Responsibility from "We've Got the Whole World in Our Hands"

In light of this parable, and as a way of thinking about the difference between its two versions, we want to trace the contours of two dominant frames that have colonized the way we think about human responsibility.

The Human-Centered Frame: Becoming Miners

Within the human-centered frame, we see ourselves as central and the rest of creation as at our disposal. According to Vandana Shiva, this frame follows from a conceptual break between our common usage of the term *resources* and what it meant before modern times. Traditionally, the notion of resource evoked the image of a spring, a source of life that arises continually and inexhaustibly. To speak of nature as a resource referenced nature's power and creativity, as well as the reciprocal relationship between humans and nature. But industrialism and colonialism gave rise to seeing humanity as over against nature, and this break transformed "a relationship of restraint and reciprocity [in]to one based on unrestrained exploitation."[3] Within this frame, humans are entitled to act on nature, which is mere scenery. Nature no longer re-sources or rises again; it is merely dead stuff that our interventions bring to life.

Shiva knows that humans have always impacted their surroundings, but she also recognizes how humanity's interaction with nature becomes a form of *mining* the earth. Humans become *miners* who no longer perceive nature primarily as the womb of a nurturing mother, but as a *container* of abundant natural "resources" to be plundered and manipulated.

In the first version of our parable, Brother Joe's interventions on behalf of the tribe demonstrate dualism's two main consequences: the desacralization of nature and the destruction of the commons.[4] Brother Joe sees the tribe as a primitive people who need a more developed way of dealing with natural "resources" through capital and technology; he

---

3. Shiva, "Resources," 229.
4. See ibid., 231–34.

does not see how the tribe enacts a cultural relationship with the river that reinvigorates their shared life.

In the technological age, we see human beings as miners. Some of us perceive that resources are neither abundant nor limited; on the contrary, they are scarce. This perception leads us from being *miners* to *managers*.

The Eco-manager Frame: Becoming Managers

To get a sense of the shift, think of the famous photo of our blue planet floating in outer space, taken by the crew of Apollo 17. This image can evoke either a heightened sense of care for and dependence upon the earth as our home, or a sense of ownership of the earth as a project that we must manage. Do we see ourselves as called to care for the earth? Or do we see ourselves as managers driven to control and regulate it?

As Wolfgang Sachs points out, the concepts "environment," "sustainable development," and "ecology" convey the same ambivalence as the "blue planet" image. All three concepts appeal to our sense of responsibility, subtly inviting us to think that we can have unlimited economic growth *and* protect the environment. What's more, all three share the assumption that the best way to deal with social and environmental problems is by embracing limits that need more and better managers.

Brother Joe's parable entails a new class of professionals who mediate between humanity and nature.[5] This managerial framework takes for granted Western expectations and remains blind to the diversity of ecological perspectives. While managers try to manage scarce natural resources, the tribe is concerned with tactics for caring for its local commons. Finding itself outside of the managerial framework, the tribe is not directly concerned about the survival of the planet. They know they cannot manage something that they cannot control.

We believe we need a new frame in which we are neither in control nor impotent. We need to hear a different tune—one that puts us in our place by taking the whole world out of our hands and by placing us back in God's hands.

5. See Sachs, "Environment," 34.

Reframing Response-ability: "He's Got the Whole World in His Hands"

The biblical narrative of creation is neither human-centered nor managerial. The spotlight is not on humanity (*adam*) alone, nor is it on the earth (*adamah*). The narrative is God-centered. God not only makes heaven and earth, but is in a free and loving *relationship* with creation. The created cosmos is good, and because God loves it so much (John 3:16), it is destined to remain in God's hands.

If creation is the theater of God's glory and the stage for this God-centered drama, the central plotline is the covenant. This means at least two things. First, creatures don't merely *exist*. To be a creature is to exist in a relationship with the Creator. Second, God's covenant is not only with humanity but also with "the earth and all its creatures."[6] Notice how dropping creation inside a "covenant with all creatures" undermines a human-centered focus without diminishing humanity as image-bearers (Gen 1:26–28). The notion of covenant also enables us to cherish the earth as God's sacred work without worshipping creation as if it were divine. What comes into view is a beautiful love triangle, or covenant, between God, humanity, and the earth and its creatures.

Through the Word, God enters into a creative dialogue with all the earth's creatures (Gen 1–2; John 1:1–5). Each creature's response-ability is its God-given capacity to respond to the call "Let there be":

"Then God said: 'Let there be light' . . . and there was light" (Gen 1:3).

"'Let there be a dome in the midst of the waters' . . . And it was so" (Gen 1:7).

"'Let the waters under the sky be gathered together into one place, and let the dry land appear' . . . And it was so" (Gen 1:9).

"'Let the earth put forth vegetation' . . . And it was so" (Gen 1:11).

"'Let the earth bring forth living creatures of every kind' . . . And it was so" (Gen 1:24).

Until God calls forth *adam*, the human earth-creature:

6. See Bouma-Prediger, *For the Beauty of the Earth*, 99.

> "Let us make humankind in our image, according to our likeness; and let them exercise skilled mastery among the other creatures" (Gen 1:26ff.).

This sequence makes clear that God calls every creature to respond: minerals, plants, and nonhuman animals all respond in their own particular ways. However other creatures respond, humans respond to the Word in trust—the "obedience of faith" (Rom 1:5; 16:26). We are called to risk *care* for the earth by "exercising skilled mastery *among* [the rest of the creatures]."[7] In the case of *adam*, the response is not simply "And it was so," but rather one determined by hearing and keeping God's word.

Yet, according to Genesis, there is a huge gap between our call as God's image-bearers and how we have wounded our response-ability. The paradoxical result of this gap between God's call and our response is that, in trying to become "like God" (Gen 3:5), we become less than human.[8] The fall is the refusal to be God's image-bearers who are response-able to God's call; this break twists God's invitation to communion into the arrogance of playing God by going beyond the limits of what God has called good.

Reframed, the environmental crisis still remains very much the work of our hands. Yet, the way forward does not lie in "powering up" and escalating our impact on the world, but rather in recalibrating it. It depends on emptying ourselves and relying on the availability of a different kind of power—God's power (Phil 2:5ff.; Rom 1:16). The ability to do so entails the recovery of response-ability, or being able to respond *to* the call of another.

Christ and the Community of Creation

In Genesis 3, we find ourselves called to respond to God and yet not being able to respond directly. Something—or someone—gets in the way.

Recall the conversation between the serpent and Eve and what happens next. God continues to call and wait for a response, asking, "Where are you? . . . What is this that you have done?" (Gen 3:9, 13). Jacques Ellul pinpoints the predicament: "Humanity now has to answer

---

7. On this translation, see Davis, "Tikkun of the Fertile Soil."

8. See Bonhoeffer, *Creation and Fall*, 111–20.

for itself, which before the break (when there was communion) was not necessary because, in a sense, God answered for them. . . . These questions put humanity in an extremely difficult situation because they really cannot respond. In order to answer truly, they would be obliged to recognize that they are now outside the communion with God, and this would imply a self-condemnation. Failing this, humanity has no choice but to give a false response, which amounts to not being fully responsible."[9] Response-ability is difficult because if we do not hear the call in trust, then we distort it. Once we distort the call, a distorted response follows.

And yet, the one who "was in the beginning with God" (John 1:2) is the same one who has "live[d] . . . by every word that comes from the mouth of God" (Matt 4:4). Christ, the true image of God (Col 1:15), "speaks the words of God and gives the Spirit without measure" (John 3:34). Only God has the power to re-create by breathing into us once more God's "spirit of life" (Gen 2:7; John 20:22). This one is also the one mediator (1 Tim 2:5) of God's call-and-response and, therefore, between a redeemed humanity and the creation-that-is-being-made-new.

So, our response begins by hearing once again the truth about image-bearing. Whereas the serpent is the one who divides, Jesus is the Savior, or the one who sews everything back together. Indeed, salvation is the sewing back together of what God joined in the beginning.

Playing the More Beautiful Music

We have not offered a technical solution but a basic response: let's delink our understanding of human responsibility from our false frames, and let's reframe responsibility as our responsibility *to* God, or the rediscovery of our creaturely response-ability.

Response-ability is not a checklist of "50 Ways to Save the Planet." Response-ability is fundamentally a matter of repentance that precedes response-ability. The Creator does not call us to be responsible for the environment. The Creator calls human beings to be response-able: to care for creation as our response to being created through and living by

9. See Ellul, *On Freedom, Love, and Power*, 78–79.

the word, as God's image-bearers within God's covenant with the whole community of creation. Are we willing to be response-able in this way?

We want to conclude by offering an alternative for how we imagine and embody human response-ability as image-bearing creatures: not with the "skilled mastery" of miners or managers, but with the skilled mastery of fellow musicians in the community of creation. To be a good group musician, you not only have to know how to play your part, but you also have to know how to play together: how to listen to the others in your midst, to be generous, alert, and even playful. You have to master playing not just for yourself, but also playing by call and response.

Martin Luther King Jr. once contrasted the captivating music of the Sirens (which leads to destruction) with the even more beautiful music of Orpheus (which guides the way forward, between the rocks of Scylla and Charybdis).[10] His point: to resist the music of the Sirens, we must hear and play the more beautiful music.

The contemporary tune of the Sirens is some variation on "We've got the whole world in our hands." This is a catchy and alluring tune because it appeals not only to our sense of responsibility, but also to our sense of justice. We hear this tune and we say to ourselves "Yes, we have got to put the world right." Presumably, the temptation to follow this tune is just as great for us as were the three temptations put before Jesus in the desert. After all, what's wrong with being environmentally relevant, spectacular, and powerful when you are doing it in the name of responsibility?

Of course, Jesus did say no to his three temptations, but as our Orpheus, his tune guides us not primarily by his no but by his yes. His song does not focus on where we should refuse to go or what we should refuse to do, but draws us close as the creation's co-composer and lead singer. Jesus is the one who knows how to play the more beautiful music: "Trust in God, trust also in me / I am making all things new" (John 14:1; Rev 21:5). Jesus is our way between the Scylla of arrogance and the Charybdis of denial. He is our exodus-in-person—not an escape from creation but a way back into it.

In the second version of our parable, we find someone who has heard and learned to play the more beautiful music. Emptying him-

10. See King, "Where Do We Go from Here?," 629.

self of his own cultural aspirations, Brother Joe takes on "the mind of Christ" (Phil 2:5) and finds himself captured by a desire to belong with the tribe. He humbly learns the tribe's wisdom and shares his own when appropriate. He shows the difference between being responsible *for* the tribe and their environment and being responsible *to* God in joining the tribe in their commons. He has learned what it means to become response-able. In him, the tribe sees a reflection of God's glory, because Brother Joe has become fully alive.

In responding to God and caring for creation, Brother Joes shows us why the music he hears and plays is more beautiful than the alternative. Ultimately, he shows us that creation is not waiting for a gang of responsibility addicts to descend en masse, intervening and announcing to the world what everybody should be doing. Joe shows us that what creation is waiting for is the revelation of "the children of God" (Rom 8:19), the manifestation of humble image-bearing creatures. Yes, all creation is eagerly awaiting for those who respond in trust and obedience to the word that sets us and the whole creation free (Rom 8:21).

10

What about Jesus and the Fig Tree? Jesus Talks to Plants—Prophetic Warnings, Agrarian Wisdom, and Earth Symbolism

Ched Myers

I AM SOMETIMES ASKED whether Jesus's "cursing" of a fig tree doesn't cut against the grain of a theology and practice of creation care and/ or nonviolence. Oddly, the question arises among both conservative Christians *and* anti-Christian environmentalists, who wonder whether this text authorizes our instrumental use (or abuse) of the earth. This essay will look at this story in its social and literary context, and then examine another teaching that gives us a much clearer insight into Jesus's actual attitude toward nature.

"Banning" Fig Tree and Temple: Prophetic Protests against Economic Exploitation as Apostasy

Both the Matthean (Matt 21:19–21) and Markan (Mark 11:12–14) versions of the fig tree "cursing" are narrated in tight relationship to Jesus's "exorcism" of the temple. I will follow Mark as the earliest form of the tradition.

On the following day, when they came from Bethany, he was hungry. Seeing in the distance a fig tree in leaf, he went to see whether perhaps he would find anything on it. When he came to it, he found nothing but leaves, for it was not the season for figs. He said to it, "May no one ever eat fruit from you again." And his disciples heard it.

Then they came to Jerusalem. And he entered the temple and began to drive out those who were selling and those who were buying in the temple, and he overturned the tables of the money-changers and the seats of those who sold doves; and he would not allow anyone to carry anything through the temple. He was teaching and saying, "Is it not written, 'My house shall be called a house of prayer for all the nations'? But you have made it a den of robbers." And when the chief priests and the scribes heard it, they kept looking for a way to kill him; for they were afraid of him, because the whole crowd was spellbound by his teaching. And when evening came, Jesus and his disciples went out of the city.

In the morning as they passed by, they saw the fig tree withered away to its roots. Then Peter remembered and said to him, "Rabbi, look! The fig tree that you cursed has withered." Jesus answered them, "Have faith in God. Truly I tell you, if you say to this mountain, 'Be taken up and thrown into the sea,' and if you do not doubt in your heart, but believe that what you say will come to pass, it will be done for you. So I tell you, whatever you ask for in prayer, believe that you have received it, and it will be yours. "Whenever you stand praying, forgive, if you have anything against anyone; so that your Father in heaven may also forgive you your trespasses." (Mark 11:12–25)

The narrative composition is what scholars call a Markan "sandwich," or framing:

- fig tree "cursed" (Mark 11:12–14)

◊ Temple "cleansed," Jesus's teaching (11:15–19)

- fig tree "withered," Jesus's teaching (11:20–25)

This rhetorical structure implies that the mysterious gesture of the outer frame and the public action of the centerpiece interpret each other. The two dramatic "prophetic actions" are each, in turn, clarified by "teachings" (11:17a and 11:22a).

These twinned episodes follow immediately upon Jesus's so-called Triumphal Entry into Jerusalem, which I have elsewhere interpreted as street theater reflecting Jesus's nonviolent messianic resistance to the hegemony of both Roman and Judean elites.[1] This sets our text firmly in a political context. After a brief "reconnaissance" of the Temple court-yard (11:11), Jesus then withdraws to Bethany. The next day, he returns to launch his actions. Let's look first at the temple protest (11:15ff.).

Jesus's target is the banking/trading class, whom he "drives out" (*ekballein*, the verb most commonly used by Mark for exorcism). Jesus could have been neither surprised nor indignant at the marketplace's existence per se, since commercial activity was a normal aspect of temples in antiquity. The issue rather was the way in which the political economy of the Temple State had become oppressive to the poor.

Jesus singles out two street-level representatives of the profitable commercial interests controlled by the high-priestly families: "money-changers" and "pigeon sellers" (11:15). The former presided over currency exchange and transaction (all pilgrim money had to be converted into Jewish or Tyrian coin before Temple dues and tithes could be paid). With revenues pouring into Jerusalem from Jews all over the Mediterranean world, these banking interests wielded considerable power. "Pigeon sellers" refers to those who trafficked in a staple commodity with which the poor met their cultic obligations (Lev 12:6; 14:22; see Luke 2:22–24). Jesus "overturns" these stations used for exorbitant profit that marginalize already vulnerable populations.

Jesus seems to have declared a "ban" on further economic activities for that day: "He would not allow anyone to carry anything through the temple" (11:16). Is this believable, given that Judean security forces and a Roman garrison stood close by to protect the orderly function of the Temple? We can best interpret this episode as a symbolic direct action signaling intent towards an end. We might say that Jesus "shut down"

1. See Myers, *Binding the Strong Man*, 294.

the Temple no more—but no less—than a modern nonviolent protest blockade temporarily "shuts down" the Pentagon.

This bold action required strong justification, which is forthcoming in Jesus's invocation of two great prophetic traditions (11:17). Jesus first appeals to Isaiah's vision of what the Temple ought to represent: a sanctuary for all peoples, especially the outcast and marginalized (Isa 56:3–8).[2] He then cites Jeremiah to illustrate what the Temple had in fact become: an institution that robs its own people (Jer 7:1–14). Jeremiah's oracle warned that unless people practiced justice toward "the alien, the orphan and the widow," the Temple would be destroyed. According to Jesus, this ultimatum has now arrived. At the conclusion of Mark's "Jerusalem controversy narrative" comes an object lesson of dispossession: the widow's mite (12:41–44). I believe this story articulates Jesus's condemnation of the Temple treasury, not a commendation of a pious woman, effectively framing Mark 11–12 with critiques of the Temple political economy.[3] In response, Jesus calls for the Temple's demise (13:2).

As noted, the fig tree story frames the Temple action. On his way to the Temple precinct, Jesus encounters a tree that is unable to relieve his "hunger" (11:12f.). He then pronounces a similar kind of "ban" on the tree: "May no one ever eat fruit from you again" (11:14). It is the *disciples*, we should note, who interpret this as a "curse" (11:21). Jesus would, of course, have known that springtime was not the "season" (Greek *kairos*) for figs. This means to signal to the reader that this is a symbolic action—certainly not an environmental one! In fact, as William Telford argues in his exhaustive study of this text, the Hebrew Bible "on the whole knows very little of nonsymbolical trees." He shows how both older and contemporaneous literature clarifies this somewhat odd "magical tale."[4]

As a prophetic sign-action, this reenacts Micah's lament over Israel's apostasy: "Woe is me! For I have become one for whom . . . there is no first-ripe fig for which I hunger. The faithful have disappeared from the land, and there is no one left who is upright" (Mic 7:1–2). This sym-

2. For an explication of this important text, see Myers, "A House for *All* Peoples?"

3 .Myers, *Binding the Strong Man*, 320.

4. Telford, *Barren Temple and the Withered Tree*, 161.

bolism is intensified after the Temple exorcism, when the disciples find that the fig tree has "withered to its roots" (11:20–21). In the Hebrew Bible the fig tree symbolized peace, security, and prosperity in Israel. The fruitful fig was a metaphor for God's blessings, while a withered tree symbolized judgment, both symbolically (see Jer 8:13; Isa 28:3f.) and as a literal consequence of war (Joel 1:7, 12).

By linking the fig tree "ban" to the Temple "ban," Mark also invokes another bitter oracle: "Because of the wickedness of their deeds, I will drive them out of my house. I will love them no more; all their officials are rebels. Ephraim is stricken, their root is dried up, they shall bear no fruit" (Hos 9:15–16). This narrative unit in Mark, then, represents an embodied political parable. The "officials" who profit from the "house" must be "driven out." "Fruitless," the Temple-State is destined to "dry up." Standing firmly within the sign-prophet tradition, Jesus uses agricultural and political metaphors to upbraid his people regarding the historical consequences of infidelity to their vocation.

The "epilogue," at first glance, seems out of place: Jesus exhorts his followers to "Believe in God!" (Mark 11:22–25). We must keep in mind, however, that the Temple represented the very heart of the Judean social order; the God of Israel resided there. The prospect of its demise would have provoked a crisis regarding national identity and viability. Jesus recognizes this as a predicament of faith and urges his disciples to believe in a world liberated from the Temple-State but still inhabited by God.[5] He then assures them that this great monolith (known in the tradition as the "mountain of the house," or "this mountain") can be overthrown. "Truly I tell you, if you say to this mountain, 'Be taken up and thrown into the sea,' and if you do not doubt in your heart, but believe that what you say will come to pass, it will be done for you" (Mark 11:23).

Interestingly, Luke, who omits the fig tree (*sukē*) action, redacts Jesus's reply by replacing "mountain" with "sycamore fig tree" (*sukaminō*): "If you had faith the size of a mustard seed, you could say to this *sukaminō*, 'Be uprooted and planted in the sea,' and it would

---

5. On "mountain" as metaphor for the Temple in the Hebrew Bible and contemporaneous literature, see ibid., 118.

obey you" (Luke 17:6).[6] This further suggests that there was a deep semantic and symbolic equivalence in the oral tradition between fig tree/mountain/temple.

Mark's phrase "be taken up and cast into the sea," meanwhile, recalls Jesus's exorcism of Legion (Mark 5:9–13), which in turn alludes to the Exodus vanquishing of Pharaoh's army (Exod 14). In other words, Mark 11:24 defines faith as political imagination: believing in the possibility of a society freed from the powers of Roman militarism and the Judean aristocracy. But what about the "indispensable" role of the Temple cult in forgiving sins? Jesus proposes to solve that problem by radically democratizing reciprocal forgiveness in community (11:25). It is little wonder that the priestly aristocracy wanted him arrested (11:27; 12:12)!

To ensure we do not miss his point, Mark returns to the Temple/fig tree theme in Jesus's apocalyptic sermon (Mark 13). That section begins with Jesus pronouncing the overthrow (Greek *kataluthē*) of the Temple superstructure (13:2). Incredulous, the disciples ask, "Tell us, when will this be, and what will be the sign when these things are all to be accomplished?" (13:4). Then, toward the end of the sermon, Jesus concludes, "From the fig tree learn the parable: as soon as its branch becomes tender and puts forth its leaves, you know that summer is near" (13:28). Indeed, the crisis of the Judean Temple State was coming to a head for Mark, writing amidst the revolt against Rome in 66–70 CE, and Jesus's fig tree symbol was meant to underscore the urgency of this *kairos*. "Who could doubt," concludes Telford, "the extraordinary impact that Jesus's cursing of the fig-tree would have produced upon the Markan reader, schooled to recognize symbolism wherever it occurred."[7]

Sadly, what is extraordinary is that so many modern Christians have not been schooled to "learn the parable of the fig tree." To use this text to authorize dominating attitudes toward nature misses the point

6. The *Theological Dictionary of the New Testament* discusses the ambiguity of *sukaminos*, which could refer either to the "mulberry tree" or "sycamore fig" (*Ficus sycomorus*), preferring the latter on the strength of the LXX of Amos 7:14 and contemporaneous literature (758).

7. Telford, *Barren Temple and the Withered Tree*, 162. On the setting of Mark's composition during the Jewish Revolt of 66–70 CE, see Myers, *Binding the Strong Man*, 344–46.

in two crucial ways. First, literalizing a Jewish parable that takes pains to present itself as richly symbolic is an error with a lamentably long and consequential history in Gentile Christendom. This arises, second, from illiteracy in the Hebrew Bible, in this case concerning not only the prophetic texts cited above, but the real biblical narrative regarding flora.

Laying Siege to the Trees or Listening to the Flowers?

That narrative is best typified by the Deuteronomist's remarkable injunction: "If you besiege a town for a long time, making war against it in order to take it, you must not destroy its trees by wielding an ax against them. Although you may take food from them, you must not cut them down. Are trees in the field human beings that they should come under siege from you?" (Deut 20:19). This reflects a scriptural ethos that unapologetically imputes intrinsic value to trees (and all living things). This ethos, first laid out in the primal story of creation (Gen 1), can be briefly summarized in a few examples.

Trees play a crucial role in salvation history. In Genesis 12:6f. Abram encounters YHWH under an oak. "The Hebrew *'elon moreh* connotes a tree with sacred associations," writes Nahum Sarna. "*Moreh* must mean 'teacher, oracle giver.'"[8] It is here that Abram pitches his nomad's tents; here that God first tells Abram of his future in this land; and here that Abram builds the first altar in the Bible. Similar scenarios occur repeatedly throughout the Abraham cycle (Gen 13:18; 15:1ff. and 18:1ff.; 21:33). The Israelite heroes Gideon (Jud 6:11) and Elijah (1 Kgs 13:14; 19:4) also had divine encounters beneath sacred trees. Clearly, this community understood its landscape and habitat as a medium for divine communion and revelation. Israel's spirituality was rooted in place.

The famous cedars of Lebanon deserve special mention here. Revered as the "trees of the garden of God" (Ezek 31:8), they are ubiquitously praised in Scripture as symbols of beauty and grandeur (for example, Ps 92:12; 104:16f.; Song 4:5; Hos 14:5–7). There is also a long tradition of prophetic protest against their destruction by ancient impe-

8. Sarna, *Genesis*, 91.

rial wars and economic exploitation (Jer 22:14f.; Isa 14:3–8; 37:23f.).[9] There is, in short, simply no biblical tradition of antipathy toward nature that could lead us to interpret Jesus's petulant destruction of a fig tree literally, much less as some sort of positive object lesson of messianic dismissiveness to be imitated.

On the other hand, both testaments are full of "symbolic trees." In the Gospels, already in John the Baptist's preaching we find the judgment metaphor of "trees bearing good or bad fruit" (Matt 3:10/Luke 3:9). This same image concludes Jesus's Sermon on the Mount (Matt 7:17–19/Luke 6:43f.). Matthew 12:33 reiterates the metaphor, which Luke clearly understood to imply a historical ultimatum on the nation and softens into a parable of patience. Jesus's severe dictum in Luke 13:5 ("Unless you repent, you will all perish") is followed by a field worker's poignant appeal for more time "for the tree to bear fruit": "A man had a fig tree planted in his vineyard; and he came looking for fruit on it and found none. So he said to the gardener, 'See here! For three years I have come looking for fruit on this fig tree, and still I find none. Cut it down! Why should it be wasting the soil?' He replied, 'Sir, let it alone for one more year, until I dig around it and put manure on it. If it bears fruit next year, well and good; but if not, you can cut it down'" (Luke 13:6–9).

Trees signify redemption as well in the New Testament, from Mark's mustard seed that grows into the greatest of trees (Mark 4:32) to John's Tree of Life (Rev 2:7; 22:2, 14).[10] For the Apostle Paul, the transformation of the cross from a "cursed" to a "saving" tree signifies our own liberation. And in Romans 11:16–24 he explores the relationship between Jews and Gentiles through the metaphor of wild olive branches grafted onto domesticated stock.

For all their social, religious, and political symbolism, however, images of flora in the New Testament remain "earthy," drawing deeply on the agrarian experience and cosmology of Palestinian agrarian culture. Such discourse reflects true "ecological literacy": the travails of dry soil farming (Mark 4:2–8), the intimate knowledge of plant succession (Jas 3:12), or seasonal impacts on cultivation (Luke 21:30; Rev 6:13).

9. On this, see Myers, "The Cedar Has Fallen!"

10. Both are political metaphors. On the former, see Myers, *Binding the Strong Man*, 179. On the latter, see Myers, "Everything Will Live Where the River Goes."

Paul's olive-grafting was already an ancient horticultural art form, one fundamental to the survival of his people. So Jesus's earth-symbols (like the fig tree) spoke powerfully to his audience of peasant farmers and arose from symbiosis with the land, not hostility to it.[11]

It is our alienated culture of modernity, having lost its sense of rootedness in place and the natural world, that gives rise to misreadings of prophetic symbols. After all, it is we who have been "making war on trees" for centuries, clear-cutting the continents and commodifying nature in ways biblical antiquity would not comprehend. And because we relentlessly exploit land for which we feel little affection or identification, earth symbolism has virtually disappeared in our churches. This must change if we are to survive the ecological endgame engendered by our way of life.

The Lilies of the Field

If the fig tree action represents a warning tale, let me conclude with a "positive" gospel teaching that can help us recalibrate. Jesus's conversation with/about the "lilies of the field" (Luke 12:27f.) stands in stark contrast, a commendation rather than a cursing. More importantly, this teaching is neither symbolic nor metaphorical, but a straightforward challenge to learn from the "alternative economy of nature."

This "lilies" passage, too, is part of a literary unit that concerns economic justice. Luke 12:13–34 consists of two contrasting object lessons. The first denounces the artificial abundance of the rich in the negative example of a landowner who can't hoard enough; it warns against the lethal, predatory force of "greed" (12:13–21). The second (12:22–34) offers twinned positive lessons from nature that reflect the divine guarantee of material sufficiency to the just. Each part concludes with parallel proverbs about "treasure" (12:21 and 34), which explicitly contrast what Wendell Berry calls "the two economies."[12] The "Great Economy" of nature precedes and will survive the "little economy" engineered by humans.

11. For two brilliant and relevant studies, see Davis, *Scripture, Culture and Agriculture*, and Hiebert, *The Yahwist's Landscape*.

12. See Berry, *Home Economics*.

Our focal text begins, "Therefore I tell you, do not worry about your life" (12:22). This is a command, not a suggestion, and warnings against socially engineered anxiety are a refrain in the ensuing teaching (vv. 22, 25, 29). To accomplish this seemingly impossible counsel we must change lenses: "Consider . . ." (12:24, 27). The Greek imperative *katanoēsate* commands urgent action; I would translate it as "Refocus your attention instead to this!"

Two examples—ravens and lilies—follow in a parallel doublet (12:24–29). Jesus is likely pointing out these object lessons as he walks through a field with his disciples. The truth is close at hand, if we pause long enough from our civilizational preoccupations to encounter what Thomas Aquinas famously called "the book of nature." Jesus is not being utopian, merely redirecting our attention to the ultimate reality in front of us: the sensuous, mystical world of the biosphere. Yet he understands that we do not have eyes to see it because we have objectified nature and are utterly preoccupied by our built environments.

The ensuing discourse is neither poetic nor transcendental; it is about our economic sustenance. The example of the raven alludes to two texts that praise God's gracious provision to all living things, particularly in times of hunger (Job 38:41; Ps 147:9). Ravens know nothing about the rich man's "storage rooms" (Luke 12:18), "but God feeds them" –and they, in turn, feed the prophet Elijah in the wilderness (1 Kgs 17:1–16)!

Jesus's second example is the wild lilies that bloomed in the Jordan Valley in spring. These flowers do not engage in hard labor, such as spinning cloth. "Yet I tell you," says Jesus with rhetorical insistence, "Solomon in all his glory was not 'wrapped around' [Greek *periebaleto*] like one of these." Referring to the sumptuous royal garb of Israel's greatest king, this is probably a euphemism for the great Solomonic temple, the zenith of Israel's civilizational aspirations. Jesus asserts that the greatest social and technological achievement known to his Judean contemporaries has less intrinsic value than one wildflower in the divine economy. What if he means it?

Yet Jesus is only invoking the ancient cosmology articulated in Genesis 1, and again in the primal tale of Exodus 16: namely, that God's creation will provision human beings—as long as we share the gifts of nature equitably.[13] Indigenous peoples the world over share this world-view, and for the vast majority of human history it animated lifeways characterized by symbiosis with nature, sustainable local production and consumption, and cooperative and equitable work patterns. The Bible simply reminds us of the oldest wisdom on the planet.

The wildflower teaches us not to "seek food and drink" (12:29) after the manner of the rich man's decadence and greed (12:19). "The nations of the world desire [Greek *epizēitei*] such things" (12:30) alludes to Roman imperial society, which was awash in anxiety, alienation, and addiction—not unlike our own. Yet Jesus is not devaluing material life by invoking some ascetic ideal. He emphasizes that God, as a nurturing heavenly parent, is mindful of our legitimate needs. The rich farmer secured his food and drink by playing the market to his advantage, but could never be sure he had enough (12:17–19). Disciples are to "seek first the Kingdom" (12:31)—which is to say, the divine cosmology of enough for everyone, and practices that cohere with it.

This conversation with the wildflowers most directly reveals Jesus's relationship to nature—fig trees included. Admittedly, for people concerned primarily with economics its counsel seems frankly absurd, its worldview the opposite of capitalism's. But the historical project of "Progress," predicated upon re-engineering nature for profit, has pushed our ecological and social systems to the brink of collapse. Do we trust in an economic worldview that sustained human life for one hundred thousand years, or one that may not last another one hundred? Or, as Jesus queried, who is the real "fool" here (Luke 12:20)?

13. On this, see Myers, *The Biblical Vision of Sabbath Economics*.

11

Isn't It All Going to Burn Anyway?
Finding Common Ground with
Creation Care Skeptics

Nancy Sleeth

IT WAS A PERFECT Saturday afternoon: cloudless sky, seventy-two degrees, and a clean breeze blowing across the mountaintop where my husband, Matthew, and I sat on a bench, enjoying the view. We had just finished leading a morning workshop on the biblical call to care for God's creation. The church sponsoring our visit was putting us up at a retreat center. I lay back on the bench. Birds serenaded us overhead, including (appropriately!) a bluebird of happiness.

A few yards away from us, a family was picnicking—three children with their parents. In between ripples of good-natured teasing and laughter, the son, about eight years old, leaned comfortably against his dad while being quizzed on Bible verses. The kid knew his stuff, and his father was clearly proud of him.

My husband made a friendly comment and began to chat with the dad. After the initial introductions, the conversation quickly turned to Scripture and matters of faith. Matthew always welcomes an engaging theological discussion and was delighted to have crossed paths with such an intelligent and devoted believer.

When asked what had brought us to the retreat center, Matthew briefly told him about our creation care ministry, Blessed Earth. The conversation stalled for a minute. Then, in a well-meaning tone, the father posed an all-too-familiar question: "If Revelation says it is all going to burn up in the end, why should Christians care?"

Finding Common Ground

While traveling the country, we've encountered many variations of this "it's all going to burn anyway" question. Why care for the earth when God's just going to destroy it? If we're ultimately made for heaven, why worry about the earth? Aren't there more important things to do, like bringing people to Christ?

Such questions can easily become divisive. A radio host recently opened his interview with my husband as follows: "When I think of environmentalists, I picture long-haired, Birkenstock-wearing hippies who rant about recycling and global warming. What do you have to say about this, Dr. Sleeth?"

A lot, actually, but not what the interviewer may have been expecting. Instead of taking the bait, we focus on the biblical call to be wise stewards of God's gifts—a value we share. Rather than getting polarized by politics, we look for common ground.

The man at the retreat center went on to say that he owns hundreds of books on the end time. Between our home and office libraries, my husband and I probably have nearly as many books on creation care. As believers in Christ, however, the three of us have much that we can agree upon: love, sacrifice, compassion, hope, joy, grace, redemption, reconciliation, and renewal are values that bind us together.

Below are some responses that we have found helpful when engaging in conversations with our brothers and sisters in Christ who—often because of what they have heard on talk shows or in political arenas—initially may be skeptical about the call to care for God's creation:

Revelation Tells Us It's All Going to Burn Up in the End,
So Why Bother Taking Care of Nature?

The answer to this seemingly logical question is actually quite simple—because the earth belongs to God, who told us to protect it.

First, consider the issue of ownership. Scripture unequivocally states that God owns all of creation. "The earth is the Lord's, and everything in it," says Psalm 24:1. In Job 41:11 God declares, "Everything under heaven belongs to me." The Apostle Paul tells us that everything was created through Christ and for him (Col 1:15–16). The earth does not belong to us, but to God—a principle that permeates all of Scripture, from Genesis to Revelation.

Since we reside on earth without claim to ownership, we are therefore tenants on God's land. As tenants, we do not have the right to act toward the earth in whatever manner we wish. Rather, we have an obligation to treat the land with the proper amount of respect due to its owner.

Why bother taking care of nature? Because it belongs to God.

Second, not only does the earth belong to God, but God also has given us the responsibility of taking care of it. In fact, one of the first jobs God gives humanity is to tend and protect the earth (Gen 2:15). This is a command, not a suggestion; it has no expiration date and is still in full effect.

But the story does not end in Genesis. Before entering the promised land, the Israelites are told that they are to provide for the "redemption of the land" (Lev 25:23–24), thus demonstrating the inherent value God places on the natural world. Likewise, Jesus himself warns his listeners to be faithful with what has been entrusted to them (Luke 16) and states that God cares when even a single sparrow falls to the ground (Matt 10:29). Our role toward God's creation is that of caretakers.

Why bother taking care of nature? Because God tells us to.

Didn't God Give Us Dominion Over the Earth?

Yes, God gave us dominion, but dominion should not be confused with license. Dominion implies great responsibility. We give teachers dominion over our children when we send them to school, but we would not be pleased if at the end of the day our children came home ignorant, battered, and bruised. The same principle applies to dominion over the earth; when God gave us dominion over the earth, God did not intend for us to destroy creation. As God's appointed stewards, we can use natural resources, but not abuse them.

Suppose you borrowed a car from somebody. Would you want to return it with cigarette butts in the ashtray, dents in the bumper, and an empty gas tank? Like the car, the earth is on loan to us. We are to pass it on to future generations in as good or better shape than we received it.

Moreover, God created the physical earth to sustain *all* life, not just humans. On the renewed earth, God specifically promises to sustain all creatures great and small: "In that day I will make a covenant for them with the beasts of the field, the birds in the sky and the creatures that move along the ground" (Hos 2:18).

Yes, we were created in God's image, and yes, we were given special responsibilities, including caring for all of God's creatures. However, dominion should not be synonymous with domination. Domination leads to reckless consumption; dominion leads to the kind of servant leadership exemplified by Christ.

If We Already Know the Earth Is Going to Burn, Why Not Hasten the End?

No one knows exactly when the end time will come, not even Jesus (Matt 24:35–37). Until then, we are all called to do God's work. As commanded in the Hebrew Bible, an important part of God's work is *abat* and *shamar*—tending and protecting the earth he placed in our care.

The prophet Amos explicitly warns us:

> Woe to all of you who want God's Judgment Day!
> Why would you want to see God, want him to come?
> When God comes, it will be bad news before it's good news,
> the worst of times, not the best of times.
> (Amos 5:18–19, The Message)

This misguided desire to hasten the end time surfaced one afternoon when a new friend invited Matthew and me to lunch. Our host, a devoted father, loved his teenaged daughter but deeply regretted that she did not have a relationship with Jesus. Yet, several times the man also stated that he prayed Christ would return tomorrow.

Matthew and I were both puzzled by this mixed message: As parents, wouldn't we want more time, not less, for Christ to open our child's heart? Shouldn't we pray that, in God's infinite mercy and grace, the end time is delayed until those we love know Jesus? And shouldn't we want to extend, not end, opportunities for people around the world to meet their savior?

In the sixteenth century, Martin Luther, the father of Protestantism, was asked what he would do when the end time came. He is reported to have answered, "Even if the world were going to end tomorrow, I would plant a tree today."

Like Martin Luther, all of us should be building the kingdom, not destroying it, until the very last moment of our personal and collective end time. Live as if judgment day is coming tomorrow, but pray that we are given as much time as possible to share Jesus with the world.

Regardless of when the end time comes, no human has the right to needlessly destroy or mar anything that God has created. In fact, the author of Revelation declares that God will destroy those who destroy the earth (Rev 11:18). Only God knows the day and the hour of Jesus' return. Only the Lord knows the manner in which God intends to create the new earth. It is not our place to hasten these events through destruction, but to give life (Matt 24:14). We are to lovingly and faithfully care for what he has made until he decides to give us a new role in the new earth—God's permanent, perfected creation.

As Christians, Shouldn't We Be Concerned with Spiritual, Not Physical, Matters?

This question quickly leads to a false dichotomy. Physical and spiritual matters are not mutually exclusive; rather, they are interdependent. For example, God gave each of us a physical body. That body is a temple that must be treated with respect: "You are not your own; you were bought at a price. Therefore honor God with your body" (1 Cor 6:19–20).

On a very practical level, proper care for our bodies requires us to also care for the earth. God gave us clean water, clean air, and healthy soil. If we want to be good stewards of our bodies, we will also have to be good stewards of the physical elements that sustain life.

Won't Everything Be Renewed at the End Anyway?

Absolutely! Revelation 21:1 and Acts 3:21 state that God intends to renew *all* things. This message is reinforced in Colossians 1:20, in which we are told that all things will be reconciled to God. Paul says in Romans 8:20–21, "For the creation was subjected to frustration . . . in hope that the creation itself will be liberated from its bondage to decay and brought into the glorious freedom of the children of God." Everything—including mountains, seas, flowers, bees, you, and me—will be renewed. This is good news, indeed!

In Revelation 21:5, God declares, "I am making all things new!" This disclosure reveals an important reality about the new earth. God intends to make all things new; God does not plan to make all new things. Revelation 21:5 also provides direction on how to interact with the natural world prior to God's renewal. Because God is making all things new, we get the honor of participating in this renewal process by protecting God's earth now. We are not passive spectators of God's cosmic design of a renewed Eden. On the contrary, we play a crucial role in God's plan. This pattern reflects one of the most common narratives throughout Scripture—that of God using humans to be God's own hands and feet in accomplishing God's purposes in this world.

Not only will everything eventually be renewed, but the Bible makes clear that even now God is actively sustaining all things: "The Son is the radiance of God's glory and the exact representation of his being, sustaining all things by his powerful word" (Heb 1:3). Likewise, Paul tells us, "[Jesus] is before all things, and in Him all things hold together" (Col 1:17). If God is even now sustaining creation, then undoubtedly the earth holds inherent value and is worthy of protection.

God currently sustains the earth, ultimately plans to renew it, and longs to use us in the process.

Aren't We Supposed to Be Worried about Saving Souls,
Not Saving Whales?

There is no greater cause for rejoicing than when a lost soul comes to Christ. The Great Commission's call to share the gospel with all nations is absolutely central to the Christian faith and should be a part of the life of every believer. Evangelism, however, is not the *only* calling of Christians; the chief end of humanity—and all of creation—is to glorify God.

Scripture is clear that creation brings God glory. Psalm 96:11–13 says, "Let the heavens rejoice, let the earth be glad, let the sea resound, and all that is in it; let the fields be jubilant, and everything in them. Then all the trees of the forest will sing for joy; they will sing before the Lord." This resounding chorus of praise comes not from human voices but from the natural world and is indicative of a world alive with God's glory. Elsewhere in Scripture, we see worship coming from the sun, moon, stars, rocks, water, fish, lightning, hail, snow, clouds, storms, mountains, hills, cattle, animals, fields, and more. Like humans, they were created by God to bring glory to God. And while I think that humans alone are created in the image of God, this does not diminish the worship that God's other creations bring to him: "The heavens declare the glory of God" (Ps 19:1).

Protecting God's creation also preserves a significant way to learn about God's character. Paul declares in Romans 1:20 that "ever since the creation of the world, [God's] eternal power and divine nature, invisible though they are, have been understood and seen through the things he has made. So they are without excuse." Here Paul is making the case that God's creation serves as an avenue for people to discover God.

The book of Job explicitly tells us to "ask the animals, and they will teach you, or the birds of the air, and they will tell you; or speak to the earth, and it will teach you, or let the fish of the sea inform you. Which of these does not know that the hand of the Lord has done this?" (Job 12:7–10). Countering our human tendency toward hubris, this passage proclaims that the natural world can offer us spiritual insight. If nature holds spiritual value in God's eye, then we should be actively protecting these sources of spiritual instruction.

Unfortunately, the world is very clear on what Christians are against, but fuzzy on what we are for. The perception that Christians don't care about pollution, species extinction, and the social and human health consequences of environmental degradation can ultimately drive people away from Christ. For example, we have heard people say they do not understand how Christians can profess to love the Creator but fail to respect his creation. Thus, our failure to take a leadership role in protecting the earth has become, for some, a stumbling block to knowing God. This problem is exacerbated when political pundits rather than Scripture become our source of wisdom.

In practice, creation care opens new doors for sharing Christ's love. My husband and I have been invited to talk about Jesus in unexpected places, including National Public Radio programs, college auditoriums, and environmental conferences. Whenever possible, we give away free Bibles to those who don't own one, enabling seekers to learn more about the scriptural call to care for the earth.

In fact, we find that turning this into an either/or equation is counterproductive. We can and should be concerned with telling others about Christ while also caring for his creation. Both callings are based on the same motivation: loving God and loving our global neighbors, including future generations.

Shouldn't we be worried about saving souls? Yes! But we should also work to protect God's creation, or we may lose the opportunity to save *any* souls.

Now, Our Question for You

Once we respond to queries like those above, we often like to ask a question of our own, which my husband first posed to a skeptical audience: If you believe in an all-powerful God, as we do, and the only purpose of life is to get into heaven, then why didn't God just have us born in heaven? Why were we born on earth?

The answer, of course, is that life on earth matters. What we do on earth matters. God created the earth and cares for it. God called it "good" and gave us the responsibility to care for it. When we care for the earth, we are participating in the work of God.

Life is not merely preparation for heaven; it is also an opportunity for us to put heavenly principles into practice here on earth. God loves to redeem, restore, and renew, and God longs to involve us in the process. God created us on earth because this is a place where we can actively participate in God's work of redemption.

A centerpiece of our faith is the resurrection of Christ. Jesus *lives*, here and now, and we are already participating in the first fruits of the new creation.

Back on the Mountaintop

Back at the retreat center, the sun was getting hotter and the kids were beginning to get restless, so my husband and his new friend wrapped up their conversation with warm wishes on both sides. As the children gathered up the picnic utensils, their father asked where Matthew was preaching the next day—a sure sign that the discussion had remained not only civil but gratifying on both sides. Though our starting points may have seemed quite different on the surface, our shared belief in Jesus and the primary role of Scripture in our daily lives allowed each to listen, to learn, and—ultimately—to love one another.

"Until we meet again, brother," Matthew said in parting.

The man extended his hand. "Yes, we *shall* meet again."

Matthew and I headed back to our cabin. Before we settled in for a delicious afternoon nap, my last waking thought was "on earth as it is in heaven." One day, God will use fire to purify the earth, and all the nations will be healed in the shade of the tree of life, watered by an unpolluted river. And it will be very, very good.

12

Is Heaven Just for Human Souls?

Laura Yordy

CHRISTIAN ESCHATOLOGY IS THE study of the "end time"—that is, the last judgment, the second coming of the Christ, heaven and hell, the consummation of the created world, and so forth. Of all the branches of theology, it is necessarily the most tentative, because humans have never experienced the end time. However, not just "anything goes," because Christians rely on Scripture and tradition to guide their understanding of God's promises. When I teach eschatology, I sometimes begin by asking students, "How do you envision the world beyond this one?" They commonly portray the end time with what we might call "happy beach-ball heaven." In this type of picture, human souls are represented as smiling round shapes floating around in some dreamy atmosphere. The glory of God shines all around like sunbeams. Like most of us, the students do not realize how what they have heard and seen over the years in church and in popular culture—with its romanticizing of individual, emotional spirituality—has shaped their imaginations.

When people ask, "Isn't heaven just for human souls?" they usually have in mind an image of heaven like the one I have described. This chapter, by contrast, scrutinizes this picture of the end time. As we will see, while the picture may reflect contemporary cultural assumptions, it does not remain true to Christian tradition. The "happy beach-ball heaven" denies two central tenets of Christian doctrine: the resurrection of the body and the redemption of nonhuman creation.

The Resurrection of the Body

In accordance with my students' pictures, many Christians nowadays seem to believe that human souls depart from their bodies at death to enter heaven, as if human bodies are disposable carrying cases for souls.[1] In the first century, however, Christians regarded human beings not as souls trapped in bodies but as embodied souls or even "ensouled bodies." Humans were seen as God-created soul-body unities. So resurrection, redemption, and reconciliation applied to the whole person.

The belief in bodily resurrection dates back to at least the Pharisees, the most popular Jewish group in first-century Palestine. Not all Jews of the time believed in resurrection; the Sadducees and Essenes, for instance, seem to have denied the possibility of resurrection (of any sort). The Pharisees, though, affirmed that at some future time, God would resurrect all the dead as part of Israel's restoration. Therefore, when the Sanhedrin confronts Paul in the book of Acts, the author writes, "When Paul noticed that some were Sadducees and others were Pharisees, he called out in the council, 'Brothers, I am a Pharisee, a son of Pharisees. I am on trial concerning the hope of the resurrection of the dead.' When he said this, a dissension began between the Pharisees and the Sadducees, and the assembly was divided. (The Sadducees say that there is no resurrection, or angel, or spirit; but the Pharisees acknowledge all three)" (Acts 23:6–8). Note that Paul not only affirms the general resurrection, but also regarded the resurrection as a distinguishing element of the Pharisees, a boundary marker between them and the Sadducees. Resurrection was associated with the anticipated restoration of Israel as a nation; God would raise the people and persons of God to new life. Resurrection was not thought to occur immediately after death; instead, while the body decayed, the spirit/soul lingered in an interim

---

1. See the Scripps Howard Foundation poll, as summarized in Hargrove and Stempel, "Most American Don't Believe in the Resurrection."

state. Bodily resurrection was the second stage of life after death, when spirit and body reunited for future life.[2]

Non-Jews of the time accepted a variety of views. Those who followed platonic philosophy regarded the body as the "prison" of the soul, a prison joyfully escaped at death. At some time after bodily death, the soul would be reincarnated in another body—either another human or a nonhuman animal depending on how they lived in the previous life. This cycle would be repeated until, eventually, the soul would escape bodily existence to reside in the purely spiritual realm of the ideal Forms.[3] Most members of the Roman Empire, however, were not Platonists. Instead, they would have adhered to some combination of religious myths and popular philosophy. Those beliefs ranged from the immortality of souls (without bodies), to a shadowy existence of spirits in another world, to a future existence of souls that had quasi-material properties. All of these non-Jewish ideas, however, upheld the finality of death; whatever happens after death, the individual self is lost forever. Christian ideas about resurrection developed amidst and in contrast to this hodgepodge of perspectives.

In 1 Corinthians 15, Paul made the earliest recorded (and most often discussed) Christian claim about resurrection. Having reaffirmed the critical notion of Jesus' resurrection and future return, he turns to the question of the resurrected body. He writes, "But someone will ask, 'How are the dead raised? With what kind of body do they come?' Fool! What you sow does not come to life unless it dies. And as for what you sow, you do not sow the body that is to be, but a bare seed, perhaps of wheat or of some other grain" (1 Cor 15:35–37). He continues some verses later,

> What I am saying, brothers and sisters, is this: flesh and
> blood cannot inherit the kingdom of God, nor does the
> perishable inherit the imperishable. Listen, I will tell you a
> mystery! We will not all die, but we will all be changed, in
> a moment, in the twinkling of an eye, at the last trumpet.
> For the trumpet will sound, and the dead will be raised

2. Wright, *Resurrection of the Son of God*, 200–206.

3. Plato lays this out most clearly in the *Phaedo*.

imperishable, and we will be changed. For this perishable
body must put on imperishability, and this mortal body
must put on immortality. When this perishable body
puts on imperishability, and this mortal body puts on immortality, then the saying that is written will be fulfilled:
"Death has been swallowed up in victory."

(1 Cor 15:50–54)

For centuries biblical scholars have debated what exactly Paul
meant by a "spiritual body." The seed-plant metaphor emphasizes transformation (a seed is nothing like the plant it becomes). On the other
hand, "putting on" imperishability stresses continuity rather than transformation.[4] The question is further muddied by the fact that, for the ancient world, "spirit" was not opposed to matter in the way we think of it.
Spiritual things were a different kind of matter, less solid than flesh but
not completely immaterial.[5] Whatever happens to the body in resurrection, Paul does *not* envision souls escaping their mortal bodies in the
Platonic sense. Instead, he emphasizes that Jesus Christ's (already accomplished) resurrection guarantees the (future) general resurrection
of the dead. Jesus's risen body presages the multitude of risen bodies at
the end time, and those bodies will be free from decay and death.

Paul's account, which accords with the Gospels and Acts, differs
substantially from both Greco-Roman ideas and Jewish beliefs in several
ways. As N. T. Wright points out, resurrection held a more central place
for early Christians than it did for non-Christian Jews. The whole new
faith hinged on Jesus's actual resurrection and its guarantee of future
resurrection for all Christians. Also, Christians focused more strongly
and more clearly on bodily resurrection.[6] So the Christian hope, while
carrying the marks of its Jewish pedigree, is a new and different vision
of God's plan for humanity.

In the second century, early church fathers such as Justin Martyr
and Irenaeus vigorously upheld the redemption and salvation of the

4. For samples of this debate, see Dunn, *The Theology of Paul the Apostle*; Bynum,
The Resurrection of the Body in Western Christianity, 200–1336; and Morgan, "The
Mother of All Muddles."

5. Russell, *History of Heaven*, 41–46.

6. Wright, *Surprised by Hope*, 53–55.

body as part of Christ's saving work. Over the next several centuries, as they tried to express their beliefs in the language common to the Roman Empire, Christians such as Tertullian and Origen sometimes added the idea of an immortal soul onto the resurrected body. God would grant the soul immortality so that the soul—along with the resurrected body—could enjoy God's presence in eternity.[7] Nonetheless, Christians never discarded the idea that bodies would be included in the resurrection, transformed in some way to escape the limits of mortality but included as part of the whole person. So the Nicene-Constantinople Creed (381 CE), the most common confession of faith among Christians across the world, still asserts that "we look for the resurrection of the dead, and the life of the world to come." Even more explicitly, the Apostles' Creed proclaims belief in "the resurrection of the body, and the life everlasting."

Christian eschatology, therefore, portrays a God-suffused new life that includes a body. As twenty-first century people, we need not get embroiled in questions about the mechanics of the process. In the Middle Ages, theologians wrestled with questions about bodies that had been torn asunder or eaten by animals.[8] How would a digested body rise again? Without denying the mystery of how resurrected bodies will resemble—or not—earthly bodies, we can still embrace God's commitment to bodily existence. Stanley Spencer expressed this idea in his painting titled *The Resurrection, Cookham* (1924–27). Rather than situating resurrection on a grand cosmic stage, Spencer framed it in a village churchyard. Deceased parishioners climb out of graves, mixing with living church members in the garden. Jesus sits in the porch, cradling babies on his lap, while the Father stands behind him. Spencer conveys that the resurrection is a continuation of God's concern and care for God's people.

God's Redemption of All Creation

In the Hebrew Bible (Old Testament), the New Testament, and Christian thinking across the centuries, God redeems the entire creation. To begin considering this, we should review how the Old Testament writers

7. Russell, *History of Heaven*, 64, 67–76.

8. Bynum, *Resurrection of the Body*, 122.

envision salvation. The Hebrew prophets' visions of hope, the ways they foresee God's total rule, are characterized by their emphasis on "this-worldly" satisfactions denied in the present order: a good and long life for individuals, the continuation of family lines, community integrity, the reclamation of the land and its continued fertility, economic sustainability, freedom from oppression and injustice, the freedom to worship and the faithfulness to do so. The prophets do not see nature and history as wholly distinct categories, but as different aspects of one category: "creation." Creation, moreover, is oriented toward a goal, and that goal is the glorification of God under God's complete sovereignty. So several Old Testament writers view the land, seas, and skies coming into the fullness of their being through God's activity and creation's praise of God. For example, Isaiah 43:30 states, "The wild beasts will honor me, the jackals and the ostriches; for I give water in the wilderness, rivers in the desert." Moreover, human obedience and the "godliness" of nonhuman creation are intertwined in the story of God's people. The faithfulness of Israel and the flourishing of the land cannot be entirely detached. On the one hand, hope in God's faithfulness to Israel always includes hope for the land's renewal and the people's return to their land. On the other hand, the people's failure to honor Yahweh results in repeated devastation of the land, exile from the land, or both. The prophet Hosea makes this clear: "Hear the word of the LORD, O people of Israel; for the LORD has an indictment against the inhabitants of the land. There is no faithfulness or loyalty, and no knowledge of God in the land. Swearing, lying, and murder, and stealing and adultery break out; bloodshed follows bloodshed. Therefore the land mourns, and all who live in it languish; together with the wild animals and the birds of the air, even the fish of the sea are perishing" (Hos 4:1–3).[9]

It is not surprising, then, that land and nonhuman animals are explicitly included in commandments for the community.[10] The pres-

9. See also Isa 24:4–5; Lev 18:26–28; Deut 6:2–3; Ezek 33:25–28; Jer 4:23–26; 5:23–25; 12:4, 7–11.

10. The literature on moral and natural ecology in the Old Testament is extensive—and increasing. Some of the best sources are Brueggemann, *The Land*; Northcott, *The Environment and Christian Ethics*; and Davis, *Scripture, Culture, and Agriculture*.

ence of land in Israel's story is vivid and constant, extending from the past, through the present, into the future. Old Testament writers, especially Isaiah, presume that God intends to redeem material creation and restore relationships within and among creation's species. For instance, the famous "peaceable kingdom" verses in Isaiah depict such a redeemed life:

> The wolf shall live with the lamb,
> the leopard shall lie down with the kid,
> the calf and the lion and the fatling together,
> and a little child shall lead them.
> The cow and the bear shall graze,
> their young shall lie down together;
> and the lion shall eat straw like the ox.
> The nursing child shall play over the hole of the asp,
> and the weaned child shall put its hand on the adder's den.
> They will not hurt or destroy
> on all my holy mountain;
> for the earth will be full of the knowledge of the LORD
> as the waters cover the sea.
> (Isa 11:6–9)

These eschatological visions in Isaiah and elsewhere in the Old Testament extend beyond arable land and livestock to land and creatures that humans do not use (for example, Job 38–39, Ps 104). If, as the prophets prayed and hoped, Yahweh would one day save and restore Yahweh's people, that salvation and restoration would necessarily include *all* of creation.

In the New Testament, different end-time visions are depicted by different authors. However, scholars generally agree that "the New Testament is definitely eschatological in one way or another."[11] The coming of Jesus, at minimum, announced the kingdom of Heaven that would contrast so sharply with human kingdoms. For some New Testament writers, such as the authors of Mark and Matthew, Jesus declared the imminent arrival of the new age; for other New Testament writers, like Luke, the coming kingdom might not be looming, but

11. Hultgren, "Eschatology in the New Testament," 69.

the kingdom is a future certainty; for still other authors, like John and Paul, Jesus inaugurated the kingdom and would come again to fulfill it. Despite these differences, all New Testament eschatologies retain striking similarities with those of the Old Testament. In Jesus' parables, in Paul, and in Revelation, the kingdom is characterized by a reversal of the present socioeconomic order, radical abundance (including food and land), peace, divine justice, eradication of evil and suffering, and the union of believers with God.

For the purposes of this chapter's title question, what's crucial about that list is how New Testament writers describe the characteristics of God's plan as encompassing nonhuman creation.[12] They can do this because Jesus is not only the head of the church, or the "author of our salvation," but Lord and God of the whole cosmos.[13] The "happy beach balls" image presumes that most of creation is lost, abandoned, or even destroyed at the end time, as if Jesus's saving activity was a very narrow beam of divine concern, bypassing everything except human souls. From a biblical viewpoint, however, we cannot limit the effects of the Christ event to his followers, or even to humanity in general. Rather, Christ's work extends the length and breadth of creation. The apostles understood Jesus to be cosmically significant as soon as they recognized him as Lord, precisely because God was the creator and ruler of the whole universe. That is to say, if Jesus were not the savior of *all* creation, he could not have been the incarnation of the Father. This understanding underlies most of the New Testament writings. In all four Gospels, heaven and earth resound with the incarnation—most graphically in Luke, where "there was a great throng of the heavenly host, praising God" (Luke 2:13) and most philosophically in the prologue to John. Jesus's sovereignty over material-spiritual reality is demonstrated in the

---

12. Douglas Moo points out that reading the Old Testament as ecologically oriented but the New Testament as void of ecological concerns is contrary to the shape of the canon: "Interpretations that drive a wedge between the Old Testament and the New Testament on the issue of the natural world fail to take seriously the unity of Scripture. A biblical-theological approach as I understand it will seek to discover ways in which the NT carries on the teaching about the created world that is so important in the OT." Moo, "Nature in the New Creation," 456.

13. Think, for instance, of the Father placing "all things" into the hands of the Son (Matt 11:27; Luke 10:22; John 3:35).

healing stories, the temptation in the desert, and the transfiguration. More specifically, the "nature miracles" demonstrate Jesus's reclaiming creation from its domination by chaos. And at Jesus's death, the cosmos shook: "darkness was over the whole land" (Mark 15:33); "the earth quaked; the rocks were split; the tombs opened and the bodies of many holy men rose from the dead" (Matt 27:52–53). Indeed, Jesus's crucifixion and resurrection transformed the entire "natural" order of earthly life: through submission to the natural *and* political forces of injustice, physical suffering, isolation, and death, Christ triumphed over them. As Oliver O'Donovan writes, "Before God raised Jesus from the dead . . . the hope for redemption *from* creation rather than for the redemption *of* creation, might have appeared to be the only possible hope." But the resurrection "tells us of God's vindication of his creation, and so of our created life."[14]

Moreover, a number of New Testament texts emphasize the unlimited scope of Christ's salvific work. Three epistles—Romans, Colossians, and Ephesians—explicitly "speak of redemption on a scale that includes the whole natural world as well as human beings."[15] In Ephesians, the writer refers joyfully and surely to God's purpose "to be put into effect when the time was ripe: namely, that the universe, all in heaven and on earth, might be brought into a unity in Christ" (Eph 1:10 NEB). Even the apocalyptic texts, commonly interpreted (in our time) as an explicit (christological) rejection of "this world," need not be read through an antimaterial lens. Recent scholars have argued that the book of Revelation expresses a hope in the renewal of the earth rather than its destruction.[16] In the context of Jewish apocalyptic texts from the same era, Revelation points to the contrast between the present age and the new age as moral or spiritual, not material.

One last comment on a key New Testament text: 2 Peter 3:10 is usually translated as "the earth and the works that are upon it will be burned up" (RSV). Steven Bouma-Prediger, however, argues convincingly that the Greek verb *heurethēsetai* is better translated "found" or

14. O'Donovan, *Resurrection and Moral Order*, 13–14.

15. Gowan, *Eschatology in the Old Testament*, 107.

16. Russell, *The "New Heavens and New Earth"*; Rossing, "River of Life in God's New Jerusalem."

"discovered." The earth and everything on it will be revealed to God and judged by God, but not necessarily destroyed.[17] Destruction of the material world is not an automatic or inevitable stage in God's salvation plan. Rather, as this and other texts indicate, the whole cosmos will be judged and transformed as creation is made new.

The point here is not that resurrection of bodies and redemption of the cosmos is the only reading of Old and New Testament eschatologies (although one would have to work hard to avoid it). It is rather that such a reading is not outlandish, primitive, or a "tree-hugging" distortion. From the very beginning, Christians have testified that God has and will redeem the entirety of God's creation—spirit and matter—through Jesus Christ. If we think about it, the "happy beach balls" image is a rather bleak, truncated reflection of the world God has created, the world God sustains, and the promised new creation. Instead, we might be better off contemplating one of the great medieval and Renaissance portrayals of paradise or the "New Jerusalem." Lucas Cranach the Elder, for example, in the *Golden Age* (ca. 1530), depicts a cozy scene of cheerful people frolicking among trees, shrubs, and animals. It is a social and earthy image, emphasizing that human bliss does not consist in rejecting the material world in favor of life with God, but in enjoying the consummation of the world in the company and worship of God.

17. Bouma-Prediger, *For the Beauty of the Earth*, 77.

13

Are There Alternative Paradigms for Creation Care?[1]

John Howard Yoder

THE TITLE ORIGINALLY ASSIGNED to me was "Christian Environmental Values." One level of "environmental values" is that of the overarching worldview held by a person or a community, in the light of which particular values and their priorities are situated and defined. Another level of study seeks to improve the adequacy with which we formulate public game rules for keeping the world viable. We work toward a stronger definition of "sustainability," and for better ways to make transparent and accountable the relations between "South" and "North." We study whether deforestation, ozone depletion, CO_2 accumulation, or the HIV virus is a greater threat to the common good. We note how rising prosperity decreases birth rates but also increases resource demands. We ask

1. This essay originated as a talk given by Yoder at the Human Values and the Environment Conference held at the University of Wisconsin Academy of Sciences, Arts, and Letters in 1992. He titled his talk "Cult and Culture in and after Eden: On Generating Alternative Paradigms," which we have changed into a question format. We have also cut some of the introductory material, which did not seem pertinent to this book, and have edited the lecture for readability. First appearing in *Human Values and the Environment: Conference Proceedings* (Report 140). Copyright © 1992 by the [Nelson] Institute for Environmental Studies at University of Wisconsin-Madison and the Wisconsin Academy of Sciences, Arts and Letters. Printed with permission.

how world market mechanisms might be more justly structured. On these levels, I can hardly propose to contribute anything new.

What seems to remain for me to offer is a loosely linked handful of smaller topics. They might be called fragments of "wisdom." They have to do with how to go on living when all the big questions are insoluble. The themes I propose to attend to are "Christian" in the setting where I see them, although I can see nothing that would keep them from being shared by Jews or by Native Americans. They are "ecclesial" in the formal sense, namely in that they take account of a value-bearing community that is neither the same as, nor in control of, the world as a whole, but they are not unique to the church. I can approach them most easily by formulating them negatively.

Why Kant Can't

It may be that no axiom is more deeply rooted in our cultural reflexes than the one which Immanuel Kant stated abstractly. We call this axiom "generalizability." It says that I should make my decisions while asking whether the maxim that guides me should guide everyone. I should consider myself the prototypical actor in the human drama. I am in everyone's shoes. For example, if I cannot promise a world without war, I should be ready to kill. Any discipline I can't ask of everyone can hardly be binding for me. Therefore, any mode of action is to be tested by asking, "What if everyone did it?"

This assumption is natural in a culture where it is thought to be true that all "people of good will" share the same values and are bound by the same fate. Since Constantine created Christendom, that "truth" has been the official self-understanding of our culture's elites. Neither the Reformation nor the Enlightenment changed that deep reflex. Yet I say we must challenge that axiom.

It would have been unthinkable for Jews since Jeremiah, or for Christians before Constantine, to think that way. They were consciously and without apology a value-bearing minority. They could never have imagined themselves as the prototypical moral actor for the entire empire. Their ethical question was, "By what axioms should we be guided when we know full well that the rest of the world will not respect them?"

The Jews called this independent value system Torah and the Christians called theirs "Good News"; the two were not as different in either substance or style as the heirs of both minorities have pretended. What they had in common was that one did not learn to know God's will by laying over current issues the grid of generalizability.

One subculture exemplifies quite well the effectiveness of not taking one's signals from "What if everybody did it?": the agriculture of my Amish cousins. While the rising costs of monster tractors, synthetic fertilizers and pesticides, fossil fuels, and bank financing have bankrupted many family farms, the Amish continue to found new colonies and restore depleted land, doubling their population and their productive acreage every generation. Their demonstration, convincingly delivered over the last century, of how low-tech sustainable cultivation can compete within a high-tech market economy, would never have been undertaken if a priori generalizability had been their first criterion.

Their first "maxim" was the conviction that God's will for human flourishing is known and carried by a specific living community, unashamed to be different from "the world." The functional measure of God's sovereignty is the community's being ready to suffer the world's scorn for the sake of obedience. The content of that "obedience" is not an abstract foundational imperative, nor a specified biblical text, but a corporate lifestyle.

The second maxim underlying Amish sustainability is one—to the historian's embarrassment—whose conceptual origins cannot be documented from the records. From the polders of Friesland to the Vistula basin, from the mountaintops of the Bernese Jura to the plain of Alsace, to the Palatinate depopulated by the Thirty Years' War, the heirs of the movement which the official reformations of the sixteenth century called Anabaptist had become, by the end of the seventeenth century (the time when the Amish submovement began), in the minds of others as much as in their own, the bearers of a special mystique of identification with the land. Non-Mennonite publishers sold farmers' almanacs by putting an Anabaptist on the cover or on the masthead. Not much later this mystical reputation led to their being especially welcomed as immigrants in Pennsylvania, the Ukraine, and later in Paraguay.

This phenomenon of mystical identification with the land has no immediately evident connection with the theological and ethical distinctives that had created the Anabaptist movement in the sixteenth century—with pacifism, refusal of the oath, believers' baptism, anticlericalism, or church and state separation. Nor do we find its grounds articulated in the hymns and prayer books of the later generations.

There would be legal hypotheses to explain this fact. In most of Europe, Anabaptists could not be citizens or own land. This gave them a special stake in being exemplary tenants, and in mobility. Their capital had to be movable—namely their livestock and their skill in farming or milling. But this kind of explanation should have applied no less in some territories to Calvinist or Lutheran (or in some Alsatian villages to Jewish) tenant farmers. Therefore, further explanation is needed.

Roman Catholic priests Michael and James Himes have argued that Christians might relate to the nonhuman creation as "thou" rather than as "it."[2] Yet they give no examples of what that would mean for raising maize or breeding cattle, for responding either to the Amazon or to the HIV virus. Can one say "thou" to a water table or an avalanche? The metaphor does not seem quite right to render the Amish mystique of knowing and loving the land and the livestock as it were from inside, suffering the drought and the plague with them. Yet it comes close.

The biblical model of a happy and empathic relation to nature is for the Anabaptist and Amish farmer the garden of Genesis 2, with human caretakers keeping order, as each species of plant and beast does its thing after its kind. Nature is not understood as jungle, thicket, or desert. The thorns and thistles of Genesis 3:17–19 do not have the last word in the homesteader's way. The earthquakes, droughts, and grasshoppers that the Hebrew prophets predicted as signs of divine visitation are the exception, not the rule. The Amish-Mennonite subcommunity's capacity to reclaim and serve the land, without irreversibly depleting the aquifers or sending the topsoil downriver, is guided by that positive vision of the garden, as well as by the previously noted (negative) maxim of disregarding generalizability.

There may well be something conflictual at stake in the fact that the garden is a more congenial vision, both for the Bible and for the

2. See Himes and Himes, "The Sacrament of Creation."

Amish, than the wilderness. The Sierra Club or John Muir kind of "nature" that one can only walk through carefully, but not inhabit, is a less congenial vision than that of Eden.

What Went Wrong

The opening story in Genesis rehearses for us a holistic vision of the human predicament, stated in economic and political terms. It is not that economic and political implications or deductions are drawn, by an intellectual operation, from a general statement about "culture" or on some other level, whether religious or intellectual. There is no bridge needed from nature to history or vice versa. Adam, humankind, is formed from the earth (*adamah*) and is at home there. The vegetation is food for man and woman, but it is also their job. The divine creative initiative is extended by Adam's being directed to name and order the animals. Rationality, language, the ordering process that makes sense out of sense data, is not something already done for humans in the timeless logic of God as a platonic super spirit or Logos, or preterhistorically decided in the eternal divine councils as the Trinity discussed in Miltonian rhythms what to do with a cosmos already destined to go wrong. It is the human, in the local specificity of history, who by naming the neighbors begins to discharge the role delegated to her and to him of ordering the garden.

This is not the kind of alien or violent "dominion" over nature that later visions of human power made of it. The garden was entrusted to us as a fundamentally hospitable context for us to serve God and one another. The fruits of the plants are fitting food, the animals are friendly neighbors (not to be eaten, in the vision of Eden); we are capable of ordering this cosmos, and its good is the same as our own.

The second strand of the ancient legend is expressed in the same idiom: One fruit, one tree, is not for us to dispose of. We are not absolute; the garden's subjection to our management is not unconditional. The order we administer is not for us to change. What is wrong with seizing the fruit of the forbidden tree is not simply that it formally disobeys an arbitrary and irrational rule promulgated by an absolute and absentee landlord. Seizing the fruit is the claim to sovereignty: "You shall be Godlike," the serpent had said.

This may be the point in the ancient cosmology where the metaphor will be most translatable to our times. Now that our finite spaceship is full, the basic notion of respecting a limit is what we least readily accept. Because we are not godlike, we must discover and yield to the laws of limits and balance that govern life; we are not free to remove vegetation or to pollute as we wish. We cannot graze goats across North Africa without making a Sahara. We cannot plow the prairies without making a dust bowl. We cannot dam the Nile, or log the rain forests or the Himalayas, or send our wastes down the sewer, without untoward surprises. To think that we are able (arbitrarily) to control the system will mean seeing the (relative) control we did have slip from our grasp. What was a fertile garden with whose natural potential we could cooperate becomes a desert peopled by weeds and thistles, demanding burdensome labor before yielding any fruit. Death is the final verdict condemning the effort to break free of the divinely intended harmony. Dust returns to dust; our final link with the soil is that having refused to harmonize with it when alive, we are reabsorbed by it when dead.

But the ancient story has yet another strand, one of which our religious traditions have made much. After being thrown out of the garden and into mortality, humankind receives a renewed promise of survival. Man's work in the field will yield food, although at the cost of sweat. To woman is given the promise of posterity, although at the cost of pain. Life will continue under the conditions of history, but that it goes on under that judgment is still a divine promise.

After that promise there is a second curse, again described in terms of ecology. Even more pointedly in the Abel/Cain story than in the garden/desert account, we see here the traces of the ancient culture clash between two phases of prehistory. Cain had been going on doing what his father was condemned to do, namely tilling the soil and offering some of its fruits in sacrifice. Therein his story prolongs organically that of Genesis 3. Abel on the other hand is a throwback, for whose profession of herdsman the earlier narration had provided no etiology (animal sacrifice is not instituted by God until Genesis 6). The shepherd who does not break open the soil, who shrewdly and submissively adapts his flock's movements to the vegetation and the watering places that Mother Earth has already provided, is somehow "closer to nature" or "less fallen," less estranged from the original Edenic covenant, than the farmer. Cain was unwilling to recognize the priority of his brother's lifestyle. Yet the narrative makes no effort to make the killing understandable by giving that kind of explanation. The killing is not retaliation or vengeance. It has no reason.

Thereby the prototypical fratricide coincides with the prototypical and perennial clash at the threshold of human history between the herdsmen and the farmers. Cain can no longer stay on the farm, because the soil that has drunk his brother's blood accuses him. The Cain story then goes on to create—within less than ten verses—all the basic components of fallen history:

- the protective threat of vengeance (which some of us call "the state");

- the city (what in Latin we call "civilization");

- what we call the arts (music);

- what we call technology (Cain's metallurgy);

- and Lamech's escalating vengeance (which we call war).

All of what it takes to have moved from the Bedouin life to high Mesopotamian culture unfolds in Genesis 4 from that first murder.

Yet this prehistory remains under the sign of grace. Cain and his sons were able to create civilization "away from the presence of Yahweh" because they had been placed, by the same God who banned them, under the protection of the threat of vengeance—the same threat that Cain's descendent Lamech was to escalate into the sevenfold vendetta.

To restate in our language what the ancient story assumed: Adam makes the transition from nature to culture; Cain from culture to war. Culture—whose root meaning is agriculture—is already morally ambivalent. It is close to nature, but not natural. It scratches open the soil, wounds the breast of Mother Earth, in order to wrest sustenance from it. It is not thereby sinful, but it is part of the price of sin. It thus becomes the occasion for fresh sin and the multiplier of its damages.

Cain's sin—and therefore my sin, for we all live ultimately from breaking open the soil—was not that he tilled and harvested. It began when he refused to recognize that his brother Abel was closer to the beginnings and closer to the God of nature. But Cain deepened that offense and estrangement, and made it irrevocable, when he chose not to share in Abel's sacrifice of a sheep from the flock. Instead, in a macabre parody of the killing of an innocent sheep, he sacrificed his innocent brother. That bloodshed made even his fields hostile to him.

Does this ancient legend in any way fit not only with the roots of ancient Near Eastern civilization but with the mess we are in? I suggest that there are technological optimists among us who still trust in our capacity to discharge the original mandate to make sense of the cosmos by naming our fellow creatures and sovereignly managing our garden. This vision, when taken alone, tends to fuse organic evolution, historical progress, biblical hope language, Hegelian hope language, and technology in one seamless myth of development that only a few years ago seemed to be the other name for "peace" or for "freedom." It is a pre-fall vision, and when fully played out it hits the ceiling of the planet's limits.

Second, some religious fatalists see the core of the problem in the original rebellion and the punishment visited upon promethean pride. We are condemned to survive by sweating it out until we die. There is neither cure nor release. The best grace concedes to us is to see this struggle as a holding operation. According to these folk, we may as well sell off what is left of nature, since if we don't burn it up the second coming will. The new earth God has promised stands in no continuity to the one we are currently wasting.

Third, prophetic critics believe Cain's sin has more explanatory power than Adam's. Cain could have and should have admitted that his sacrifice was ambivalent—that his use of the earth was more violative than Abel's. The fundamental sin is not pride alone, as the Augustinians would have it, though when we speak of the inner structure of the human person we can say that that was what opened the door. The worse offense was the breach of fraternity with the simpler shepherd brother whose living from the land, like his sacrifice, was more natural. That breach resulted from the refusal to recognize that our toil in the fields, even when blessed with fruit, was already morally ambivalent, already blemished by the expulsion from Eden.

Yet even that wounded pride, and even the tension between the brothers that it produced, would not have been our downfall. Our downfall was that the pride became murder. From the levels of culture and cult we escalated the scandal to the denial of community, deceiving and destroying the brother because he was other. (More recently we have been challenged to work at the offense of the other when the difference is race, gender, or class. It may be important that the first other was not the alien but the brother—that is, the root hostility was not defined by any outward difference).

I have been looking in the Genesis legend for the presence of the agenda of culture and nature. It is there. The primal transition from gathering to shepherding to gardening, and from there to building cities and then empires, will be run through again and again as we seek to respond to the challenges we are studying here.

Yet the reason we have the story before us, the reason this ancient literature exists, is that those who recited it for generations and then wrote it down saw these prototypical events as having occurred in the providential context of divine ordering. Divine enabling is present not only in providing the first Eden, as seems to be taken for granted by many of those for whom "nature" and "creation" are equated. The intent of the expulsion from the garden (instead of death) is protective; the new beginning under changed conditions and a renewed promise is again grace. The mark that saved Cain from being the victim of vigilantes is again grace, even though the vindictive reflex which that mark symbolized opened the door for escalated vengeance.

Reviewing the lay of the land as thus classically portrayed, my response by way of suggested directions for hope can only be a pair of fragmentary insights, pebbles picked up midstream.

Does "History" Have to Be Empire?

Christian theologian and Native American George Tinker sharpens a perennial polarity.[3] Tinker argues that the barbarian invasions from

3. See Tinker, "Spirituality, Native American Personhood, Sovereignty and

Renaissance Europe, overrunning both Asia and the Americas, entailed the intrusion of a time-oriented vision of God's rule as purposive, directional, and history-making, into a world without that vision of directional history. Western liberation theologies partake no less of this linear intrusiveness than do the imperial establishment ideologies; both "liberation" and "conservation" use "God who acts" language. Both can justify empire.

This time-oriented, "God acting" vision invaded a space-oriented, inclusive vision of human dignity in the world within a divine presence. That prior, spatial vision is "just as adequate, and perhaps more satisfying and certainly more egalitarian than the West's."[4] This pre-Columbian vision of harmonious space was overrun by the European vision of linear conquest not because the immigrant culture, structured as nation-states, was more humane or more moral, but because of its superior firepower, and because of the short-range tactical advantage that can always be seized by not fighting fairly. The European intruders refused to apply to the original inhabitants the theory of human dignity to which our nation's founding documents later were to appeal.

Having stated the claim for the moral equiprobability of the pre-invasion vision, Tinker proceeds, since his context is Christian, to review how a creation-friendly restructuring of biblical language might work. He disavows "the value-neutral creation theology of Matthew Fox" and "new-age spirituality" in favor of a "'theology of community' that must generate a consistent interest in justice and peace. . . . The oppression we have experienced is intimately linked to the way the immigrants pray and how they understand . . . their relation to creation and Creator."[5]

This is not the place to converse in detail about this suggested alternative formulation. I cite Tinker only as an instance of the much more broadly represented notion, classically formulated a generation ago by Lynn White, that what went wrong in our past was the basic biblical vision of a God who acts to bring about a new history.[6] It is

---

Solidarity."

4. Ibid., 317. Tinker means the hunters and farmers of North America; he is not describing the Aztecs or the Incas.

5. Ibid., 321, 322.

6. See White, "The Historical Roots of Our Ecologic Crisis."

formulated here in culture-to-culture terms, although of course it has close analogies in the gender agenda, as in other social justice arenas. It is important for our conversation that this critique should have been stated by Tinker in the form of an appeal to an old and viable culture and history, namely his own, rather than our meeting it as we more often do in history-less trendy or fanciful forms.

This polarity is so fundamental that it would seem prima facie that there can hardly be any place to stand from where to discuss it further, to say nothing of adjudicating it. This debate, in addition to being petitionary, is relevant only to the past. Neither vision—neither that of the God who acts to cover the earth with a European-managed, satellite-linked system of farms, mines, stock exchanges, and factories, nor that of Grandmother Earth in whom we all live and move and have our being—throws any useful light on what to do about Calcutta, Cairo, or Mexico City tomorrow. Both visions fail when they collide with the finitude of the overpopulated planet. Both visions appeared quite viable until World War I, and as Tinker (I think rightly) says, the short-range victory of the Hebraic-European competitor since then has not been won on moral grounds. Neither however is viable in the modern world in the face of population growth and resource depletion; both would (and do, and will) let the children starve. Neither model as we know it can cope with the population crisis.

I can make but one fragmentary, marginal suggestion, arising from this glimpse of the hopelessness of the debate hitherto. It is that when the global system is out of control, the normal moral decency that is within our reach may matter more than the vision of a universal solution that is not. George F. Kennan said this once about superpower diplomacy. The same observation may be applied both to institutional systems (the New Economic Order) and to cultural ones (whether to prefer Grandmother Earth or Yahweh-who-acts). The clash between the European immigrants and the original inhabitants of this hemisphere would have had to come out differently if both sides had listened to William Penn, had renounced recourse to lethal arms, and had constituted mediation panels.[7]

7. See William Penn's 1681 letter to the Delaware Indians, in Marrin, *War and the Christian Conscience*, 199–201.

If Jesus of Nazareth culminates the story of Yahweh-who-acts, then Constantine and Charlemagne do not. Then we don't let Columbus, or the Columbus backlash, dictate our agenda. William Penn extrapolated that reconciling history—the one marked by Jesus and Saint Francis and George Fox—to the New World, as Columbus did not. There are thus more resources for system criticism and the discovery of alternatives within the Hebraic stream of affirming history than the Spanish empire represented. There are surely also resources for internal system criticism within Tinker's Grandmother Earth culture, but I am not qualified to say how. Seeking within each setting the potential for self-restraint is a more promising common exercise than debating which prior history was less destructive.

Using weapons is not wrong merely because the Torah prohibits bloodshed or the gospel prohibits enmity. Weapon-use is wrong because it resolves conflicts on other grounds than the nature of the problem and the dignity of all the parties involved (including not only the human adversaries, but also the trees). To renounce violence is the first functional meaning of affirming creation or nature. To renounce violence in itself solves few problems, but it holds them open for solution.

What Is Imperative Is Not Necessary

A major, still unresolved challenge in the study of ancient faith documents is what we should do with literature of the genre that the experts call "apocalyptic." A century ago, Albert Schweitzer reoriented the study of Jesus by demonstrating that it is impossible to peel off from the Gospel stories the "apocalyptic" husk, so as to leave as kernel a timeless message about God and the soul that modern readers could welcome as reinforcing ideas they already have. But how that "apocalyptic" perspective should be appropriated today is a challenge we are far from resolving adequately. As before, I can perhaps best make my point negatively, and formally.

One function of the language of apocalypse in the faith community is that it restrains the presumptuous claim to have mastered the world system, either intellectually by a set of explanations or practically by a set of power manipulations. Modern technology comes closer to "mastering" some of the angles of the way the world works, but thereby it sets loose a larger set of surprising imponderables. It is culturally good for us that the promethean myth, which describes so well our technological culture's temptations and vulnerability, should be ancient. Neither the idea that we might master the secrets of physical causation, nor the awareness that when we think we have done that, it merely escalates the destructiveness of our errors and ignorance, is a new insight.

Apocalypse promises, to those who cower under the threats of the tyrants, that tyranny will not have the last word. It promises that the wholesome potential of creation will one day be fulfilled. It promises that diversity, and even conflict, will enrich human existence rather than destroy it. The particular cosmology, or the particular vision of miracle, in which these promises were clothed in ancient times, cannot be extrapolated literally from that century to ours; but it was not meant literally then either. It was meant as a call to creative response, denying the last word to a closed-system of determinism. Some interpreters of "apocalyptic" transpose the language of promise into psychology, making of "hope" the human quality of hopefulness or optimism. Others use the language of sociology, describing the resistance of a beleaguered tribe to assimilation. Others use more intellectual equivalents: They suggest that what apocalypse communicates is "transcendence," or the notion of a God active in history. Each of these transpositions aims at enhancing the visions' accessibility or credibility. Each makes a valid point. Each is a reduction. Each of them sends us down a different path, if we ask philosophically how to validate it.

There is nothing wrong with reductionism, as long as it does not claim that its grid is the only one to use. The "remainder" that no reduction may be permitted to do away with is the good news that the future is not exhaustively contained in the past. What must be and what has to be are not the same. Fatalism as a view of the human condition cannot be falsified on the basis of the past. It is always a priori evident that "you can't get there from here." Yet "apocalypse" refuses that restriction of the data.

The viability of our culture, as we hit the ceiling of the planet's capacity, will be correlative with our finding ways for our time, as heirs of the apocalyptic hopes of all time, to envision the world that needs to be, on other grounds than that it is the necessary product of our past.

14

If You Want to Cultivate Peace, Protect Creation

Message of Pope Benedict XVI for the Celebration of the World
Day of Peace, January 1, 2010[1]

1. AT THE BEGINNING of this New Year, I wish to offer heartfelt greetings of peace to all Christian communities, international leaders, and people of good will throughout the world. For this XLIII World Day of Peace I have chosen the theme: If You Want to Cultivate Peace, Protect Creation. Respect for creation is of immense consequence, not least because "creation is the beginning and the foundation of all God's works,"[2] and its preservation has now become essential for the pacific coexistence of mankind. Man's inhumanity to man has given rise to numerous threats to peace and to authentic and integral human development—wars, international and regional conflicts, acts of terrorism, and violations of human rights. Yet no less troubling are the threats arising from the neglect—if not downright misuse—of the earth and the natural goods that God has given us. For this reason, it is imperative that mankind renew and strengthen "that covenant between human beings

---

1. Published with permission from Libreria Editrice Vaticana, which owns the copyright to this message.

2. *Catechism of the Catholic Church*, §198.

and the environment, which should mirror the creative love of God, from whom we come and towards whom we are journeying."[3]

2. In my Encyclical *Caritas in Veritate*, I noted that integral human development is closely linked to the obligations which flow from man's relationship with the natural environment. The environment must be seen as God's gift to all people, and the use we make of it entails a shared responsibility for all humanity, especially the poor and future generations. I also observed that whenever nature, and human beings in particular, are seen merely as products of chance or an evolutionary determinism, our overall sense of responsibility wanes.[4] On the other hand, seeing creation as God's gift to humanity helps us understand our vocation and worth as human beings. With the psalmist, we can exclaim with wonder: "When I look at your heavens, the work of your hands, the moon and the stars which you have established; what is man that you are mindful of him, and the son of man that you care for him?" (Ps 8:4–5). Contemplating the beauty of creation inspires us to recognize the love of the Creator, that Love which "moves the sun and the other stars."[5]

3. Twenty years ago, Pope John Paul II devoted his Message for the World Day of Peace to the theme: Peace with God the Creator, Peace with All of Creation. He emphasized our relationship, as God's creatures, with the universe all around us. "In our day," he wrote, "there is a growing awareness that world peace is threatened . . . also by a lack of *due respect for nature.*" He added that "*ecological awareness*, rather than being downplayed, needs to be helped to develop and mature, and find fitting expression in concrete programmes and initiatives."[6] Previous popes had spoken of the relationship between human beings and the environment. In 1971, for example, on the eightieth anniversary of Leo XIII's Encyclical *Rerum Novarum*, Paul VI pointed out that "by an ill-considered exploitation of nature (man) risks destroying it and becoming in his turn the victim of this degradation." He added that "not only is the material environment becoming a permanent menace—pol-

3. Benedict XVI, "Human Family, a Community of Peace," §7.

4. Benedict XVI, *Caritas in Veritate,* §48.

5. Dante, *Paradise*, XXXIII, 145.

6. John Paul II, "Peace with God the Creator," §1.

lution and refuse, new illnesses and absolute destructive capacity—but the human framework is no longer under man's control, thus creating an environment for tomorrow which may well be intolerable. This is a wide-ranging social problem which concerns the entire human family."[7]

4. Without entering into the merit of specific technical solutions, the Church is nonetheless concerned, as an "expert in humanity," to call attention to the relationship between the Creator, human beings and the created order. In 1990 John Paul II had spoken of an "ecological crisis" and, in highlighting its primarily ethical character, pointed to the "urgent moral need for a new solidarity."[8] His appeal is all the more pressing today, in the face of signs of a growing crisis which it would be irresponsible not to take seriously. Can we remain indifferent before the problems associated with such realities as climate change, desertification, the deterioration and loss of productivity in vast agricultural areas, the pollution of rivers and aquifers, the loss of biodiversity, the increase of natural catastrophes and the deforestation of equatorial and tropical regions? Can we disregard the growing phenomenon of "environmental refugees," people who are forced by the degradation of their natural habitat to forsake it—and often their possessions as well—in order to face the dangers and uncertainties of forced displacement? Can we remain impassive in the face of actual and potential conflicts involving access to natural resources? All these are issues with a profound impact on the exercise of human rights, such as the right to life, food, health and development.

5. It should be evident that the ecological crisis cannot be viewed in isolation from other related questions, since it is closely linked to the notion of development itself and our understanding of man in his relationship to others and to the rest of creation. Prudence would thus dictate a profound, long-term review of our model of development, one which would take into consideration the meaning of the economy and its goals with an eye to correcting its malfunctions and misapplications. The ecological health of the planet calls for this, but it is also demanded by the cultural and moral crisis of humanity whose symptoms have for

7. Paul VI, *Octogesima Adveniens*, §21.

8. John Paul II, "Peace with God the Creator," §10

some time been evident in every part of the world.[9] Humanity needs a profound cultural renewal; it needs to rediscover those values which can serve as the solid basis for building a brighter future for all. Our present crises—be they economic, food-related, environmental or social—are ultimately also moral crises, and all of them are interrelated. They require us to rethink the path which we are travelling together. Specifically, they call for a lifestyle marked by sobriety and solidarity, with new rules and forms of engagement, one which focuses confidently and courageously on strategies that actually work, while decisively rejecting those that have failed. Only in this way can the current crisis become an opportunity for discernment and new strategic planning.

6. Is it not true that what we call "nature" in a cosmic sense has its origin in "a plan of love and truth"? The world "is not the product of any necessity whatsoever, nor of blind fate or chance. . . . The world proceeds from the free will of God; he wanted to make his creatures share in his being, in his intelligence, and in his goodness."[10] The book of Genesis, in its very first pages, points to the wise design of the cosmos: it comes forth from God's mind and finds its culmination in man and woman, made in the image and likeness of the Creator to "fill the earth" and to "have dominion over" it as "stewards" of God himself (cf. Gen 1:28). The harmony between the Creator, mankind and the created world, as described by Sacred Scripture, was disrupted by the sin of Adam and Eve, by man and woman, who wanted to take the place of God and refused to acknowledge that they were his creatures. As a result, the work of "exercising dominion" over the earth, "tilling it and keeping it," was also disrupted, and conflict arose within and between mankind and the rest of creation (cf. Gen 3:17–19). Human beings let themselves be mastered by selfishness; they misunderstood the meaning of God's command and exploited creation out of a desire to exercise absolute domination over it. But the true meaning of God's original command, as the book of Genesis clearly shows, was not a simple conferral of authority, but rather a summons to responsibility. The wisdom of the ancients had recognized that nature is not at our disposal as "a heap of scat-

9. Cf. Benedict XVI, *Caritas in Veritate*, §32.
10. *Catechism of the Catholic Church*, §295.

tered refuse."[11] Biblical Revelation made us see that nature is a gift of the Creator, who gave it an inbuilt order and enabled man to draw from it the principles needed to "till it and keep it" (cf. Gen 2:15).[12] Everything that exists belongs to God, who has entrusted it to man, albeit not for his arbitrary use. Once man, instead of acting as God's co-worker, sets himself up in place of God, he ends up provoking a rebellion on the part of nature, "which is more tyrannized than governed by him."[13] Man thus has a duty to exercise responsible stewardship over creation, to care for it and to cultivate it.[14]

7. Sad to say, it is all too evident that large numbers of people in different countries and areas of our planet are experiencing increased hardship because of the negligence or refusal of many others to exercise responsible stewardship over the environment. The Second Vatican Ecumenical Council reminded us that "God has destined the earth and everything it contains for all peoples and nations."[15] The goods of creation belong to humanity as a whole. Yet the current pace of environmental exploitation is seriously endangering the supply of certain natural resources not only for the present generation, but above all for generations yet to come.[16] It is not hard to see that environmental degradation is often due to the lack of far-sighted official policies or to the pursuit of myopic economic interests, which then, tragically, become a serious threat to creation. To combat this phenomenon, economic activity needs to consider the fact that "every economic decision has a moral consequence"[17] and thus show increased respect for the environment. When making use of natural resources, we should be concerned for their protection and consider the cost entailed—environmentally and socially—as an essential part of the overall expenses incurred. The international community and national governments are responsible for

11. Heraclitus of Ephesus (ca. 535–ca. 475 BC), Fragment 22B124, cited in Diels and Kranz, *Die Fragmente der Vorsokratiker.*

12. Cf. Benedict XVI, *Caritas in Veritate*, §48.

13. John Paul II, *Centesimus Annus*, §37.

14. Cf. Benedict XVI, *Caritas in Veritate*, §50.

15. Paul VI, *Gaudium et Spes*, §69.

16. Cf. John Paul II, *Sollicitudo Rei Socialis*, §34.

17. Benedict XVI, *Caritas in Veritate*, §37.

sending the right signals in order to combat effectively the misuse of the environment. To protect the environment, and to safeguard natural resources and the climate, there is a need to act in accordance with clearly defined rules, also from the juridical and economic standpoint, while at the same time taking into due account the solidarity we owe to those living in the poorer areas of our world and to future generations.

8. *A greater sense of intergenerational solidarity* is urgently needed. Future generations cannot be saddled with the cost of our use of common environmental resources. "We have inherited from past generations, and we have benefited from the work of our contemporaries; for this reason we have obligations towards all, and we cannot refuse to interest ourselves in those who will come after us, to enlarge the human family. Universal solidarity represents a benefit as well as a duty. *This is a responsibility that present generations have towards those of the future*, a responsibility that also concerns individual States and the international community."[18] Natural resources should be used in such a way that immediate benefits do not have a negative impact on living creatures, human and not, present and future; that the protection of private property does not conflict with the universal destination of goods;[19] that human activity does not compromise the fruitfulness of the earth, for the benefit of people now and in the future. In addition to a fairer sense of intergenerational solidarity there is also an urgent moral need for a renewed sense of intragenerational solidarity, especially in relationships between developing countries and highly industrialized countries: "the international community has an urgent duty to find institutional means of regulating the exploitation of non-renewable resources, involving poor countries in the process, in order to plan together for the future."[20] *The ecological crisis shows the urgency of a solidarity which embraces time and space*. It is important to acknowledge that among the causes of the present ecological crisis is the historical responsibility of the industrialized countries. Yet the less developed countries, and emerging countries in particular, are not exempt from their own responsibilities with regard

18. Pontifical Council for Justice and Peace, *Compendium of the Social Doctrine of the Church*, §467; cf. Paul VI, *Populorum Progressio*, §17.

19. Cf. John Paul II, *Centesimus Annus*, §30–31, §43

20. Benedict XVI, *Caritas in Veritate*, §49.

to creation, for the duty of gradually adopting effective environmental measures and policies is incumbent upon all. This would be accomplished more easily if self-interest played a lesser role in the granting of aid and the sharing of knowledge and cleaner technologies.

9. To be sure, among the basic problems which the international community has to address is that of energy resources and the development of joint and sustainable strategies to satisfy the energy needs of the present and future generations. This means that technologically advanced societies must be prepared to encourage more sober lifestyles, while reducing their energy consumption and improving its efficiency. At the same time there is a need to encourage research into, and utilization of, forms of energy with lower impact on the environment and "a world-wide redistribution of energy resources, so that countries lacking those resources can have access to them."[21] The ecological crisis offers an historic opportunity to develop a common plan of action aimed at orienting the model of global development towards greater respect for creation and for an integral human development inspired by the values proper to charity in truth. I would advocate the adoption of a model of development based on the centrality of the human person, on the promotion and sharing of the common good, on responsibility, on a realization of our need for a changed lifestyle, and on prudence, the virtue which tells us what needs to be done today in view of what might happen tomorrow.[22]

10. A sustainable comprehensive management of the environment and the resources of the planet demands that human intelligence be directed to technological and scientific research and its practical applications. The "new solidarity" for which John Paul II called in his Message for the 1990 World Day of Peace[23] and the "global solidarity" for which I myself appealed in my Message for the 2009 World Day of Peace[24] are essential attitudes in shaping our efforts to protect creation through a better internationally coordinated management of the earth's resources, particularly today, when there is an increasingly clear link

21. Ibid.
22. Cf. Saint Thomas Aquinas, *S. Th.*, II–II, q. 49, 5.
23. Cf. John Paul II, "Peace with God the Creator."
24. Cf. Benedict XVI, "Fighting Poverty to Build Peace."

between combatting environmental degradation and promoting an integral human development. These two realities are inseparable, since "the integral development of individuals necessarily entails a joint effort for the development of humanity as a whole."[25] At present there are a number of scientific developments and innovative approaches which promise to provide satisfactory and balanced solutions to the problem of our relationship to the environment. Encouragement needs to be given, for example, to research into effective ways of exploiting the immense potential of solar energy. Similar attention also needs to be paid to the worldwide problem of water and to the global water cycle system, which is of prime importance for life on earth and whose stability could be seriously jeopardized by climate change. Suitable strategies for rural development centered on small farmers and their families should be explored, as well as the implementation of appropriate policies for the management of forests, for waste disposal and for strengthening the linkage between combatting climate change and overcoming poverty. Ambitious national policies are required, together with a necessary international commitment which will offer important benefits especially in the medium and long term. There is a need, in effect, to move beyond a purely consumerist mentality in order to promote forms of agricultural and industrial production capable of respecting creation and satisfying the primary needs of all. The ecological problem must be dealt with not only because of the chilling prospects of environmental degradation on the horizon; the real motivation must be the quest for authentic worldwide solidarity inspired by the values of charity, justice and the common good. For that matter, as I have stated elsewhere, "technology is never merely technology. It reveals man and his aspirations towards development; it expresses the inner tension that impels him gradually to overcome material limitations. Technology in this sense is a response to God's command to till and keep the land (cf. Gen 2:15) that he has entrusted to humanity, and it must serve to reinforce the covenant between human beings and the environment, a covenant that should mirror God's creative love."[26]

25. Paul VI, *Populorum Progressio*, §43.
26. Benedict XVI, *Caritas in Veritate*, §69.

11. It is becoming more and more evident that the issue of environmental degradation challenges us to examine our lifestyle and the prevailing models of consumption and production, which are often unsustainable from a social, environmental and even economic point of view. We can no longer do without a real change of outlook which will result in *new lifestyles*, "in which the quest for truth, beauty, goodness and communion with others for the sake of common growth are the factors which determine consumer choices, savings and investments."[27] Education for peace must increasingly begin with far-reaching decisions on the part of individuals, families, communities and states. We are all responsible for the protection and care of the environment. This responsibility knows no boundaries. In accordance with the *principle of subsidiarity* it is important for everyone to be committed at his or her proper level, working to overcome the prevalence of particular interests. A special role in raising awareness and in formation belongs to the different groups present in civil society and to the non-governmental organizations which work with determination and generosity for the spread of ecological responsibility, responsibility which should be ever more deeply anchored in respect for "human ecology." The media also have a responsibility in this regard to offer positive and inspiring models. In a word, concern for the environment calls for a broad global vision of the world; a responsible common effort to move beyond approaches based on selfish nationalistic interests towards a vision constantly open to the needs of all peoples. We cannot remain indifferent to what is happening around us, for the deterioration of any one part of the planet affects us all. Relationships between individuals, social groups and states, like those between human beings and the environment, must be marked by respect and "charity in truth." In this broader context one can only encourage the efforts of the international community to ensure progressive disarmament and a world free of nuclear weapons, whose presence alone threatens the life of the planet and the ongoing integral development of the present generation and of generations yet to come.

12. *The Church has a responsibility towards creation*, and she considers it her duty to exercise that responsibility in public life, in order to protect earth, water and air as gifts of God the Creator meant for every-

27. John Paul II, *Centesimus Annus*, §36.

one, and above all to save mankind from the danger of self-destruction. The degradation of nature is closely linked to the cultural models shaping human coexistence: consequently, "when 'human ecology' is respected within society, environmental ecology also benefits."[28] Young people cannot be asked to respect the environment if they are not helped, within families and society as a whole, to respect themselves. The book of nature is one and indivisible; it includes not only the environment but also individual, family and social ethics.[29] Our duties towards the environment flow from our duties towards the person, considered both individually and in relation to others.

Hence I readily encourage efforts to promote a greater sense of ecological responsibility which, as I indicated in my Encyclical *Caritas in Veritate*, would safeguard an authentic "human ecology" and thus forcefully reaffirm the inviolability of human life at every stage and in every condition, the dignity of the person and the unique mission of the family, where one is trained in love of neighbor and respect for nature.[30] There is a need to safeguard the human patrimony of society. This patrimony of values originates in and is part of the natural moral law, which is the foundation of respect for the human person and creation.

13. Nor must we forget the very significant fact that many people experience peace and tranquility, renewal and reinvigoration, when they come into close contact with the beauty and harmony of nature. There exists a certain reciprocity: as we care for creation, we realize that God, through creation, cares for us. On the other hand, a correct understanding of the relationship between man and the environment will not end by absolutizing nature or by considering it more important than the human person. If the Church's magisterium expresses grave misgivings about notions of the environment inspired by ecocentrism and biocentrism, it is because such notions eliminate the difference of identity and worth between the human person and other living things. In the name of a supposedly egalitarian vision of the "dignity" of all living creatures, such notions end up abolishing the distinctiveness and superior role of human beings. They also open the way to a new pantheism tinged with

28. Benedict XVI, *Caritas in Veritate*, §51.

29. Cf. ibid., §15, §51.

30. Cf. ibid., §28, §51, §61; John Paul II, *Centesimus Annus*, §38, §39.

neo-paganism, which would see the source of man's salvation in nature alone, understood in purely naturalistic terms. The Church, for her part, is concerned that the question be approached in a balanced way, with respect for the "grammar" which the Creator has inscribed in his handiwork by giving man the role of a steward and administrator with responsibility over creation, a role which man must certainly not abuse, but also one which he may not abdicate. In the same way, the opposite position, which would absolutize technology and human power, results in a grave assault not only on nature, but also on human dignity itself.[31]

14. *If you want to cultivate peace, protect creation.* The quest for peace by people of good will surely would become easier if all acknowledge the indivisible relationship between God, human beings and the whole of creation. In the light of divine Revelation and in fidelity to the Church's Tradition, Christians have their own contribution to make. They contemplate the cosmos and its marvels in light of the creative work of the Father and the redemptive work of Christ, who by his death and resurrection has reconciled with God "all things, whether on earth or in heaven" (Col 1:20). Christ, crucified and risen, has bestowed his Spirit of holiness upon mankind, to guide the course of history in anticipation of that day when, with the glorious return of the Saviour, there will be "new heavens and a new earth" (2 Pet 3:13), in which justice and peace will dwell for ever. Protecting the natural environment in order to build a world of peace is thus a duty incumbent upon each and all. It is an urgent challenge, one to be faced with renewed and concerted commitment; it is also a providential opportunity to hand down to coming generations the prospect of a better future for all. May this be clear to world leaders and to those at every level who are concerned for the future of humanity: the protection of creation and peacemaking are profoundly linked! For this reason, I invite all believers to raise a fervent prayer to God, the all-powerful Creator and the Father of mercies, so that all men and women may take to heart the urgent appeal: *If you want to cultivate peace, protect creation.*

From the Vatican, December 8, 2009

---

31. Cf. Benedict XVI, *Caritas in Veritate*, §70.

Afterword

William Willimon

I DON'T KNOW ABOUT you, but this book and its essays have been for me an experience in judgment. Adjudication of one's life and thought is an all-too-rare experience for a Mainline (rapidly becoming sidelined) Protestant Christian like me. On Sundays my church family seems to enjoy being told that we are people in need of great love and care, that we are gradually making upward moral progress, and that we are, when all is said and done, doing the best we can. We are the center and the crowning point of creation.

A Faith Encompassing All Creation has reminded me of how easy it is for a comfortable, affluent North American Christian like me to get the gospel wrong, to use and abuse rather than love creation, and to live as if my life is self-constructed rather than a part of God's gracious web of creativity. The modern world has deceived us into thinking that we are accountable to no standard of judgment other than our own conscience, answerable to no one but the omnivorous, sovereign self.

Jesus told a parable about a master who, on his way out of town on a journey of indeterminate duration, calls his underlings in and dumps upon them his entire net worth (Matt 25:14–30). Without any instruction in how to care for his wealth, he hands over to them a vast treasure.

We preachers love this story as the Parable of the Talents, focusing our attention upon the success or failure of the servants' investments of the gifts they have been given. My congregations have always liked that sort of sermon, finding it wonderfully self-flattering: we are incredibly talented, gifted folk who have a responsibility to use our talents wisely.

In *A Faith Encompassing All Creation*, gifted theologians have reminded us of the mischief worked by that interpretation of the parable—we've got a God-given responsibility to use the world and its resources to our advantage without counting the cost.

But after these essays have had their way with me, I'm hearing this parable not as a parable about me and my talents but rather as a story about God's gifts and God's judgment. What sort of God have we got? Jesus depicts a God who is incredibly generous, almost absurdly so, giving into our hands a creation we didn't fabricate or deserve. With a minimum of commands and demands we've been given quite a world.

But as the Germans say, every gift (*Gabe*) entails an assignment (*Aufgabe*). God loves us enough not only to be the gracious giver but also to be the gracious judge. We are held accountable. For all of us, according to the gospel, there will be a time of reckoning. Of all of us, the Judge will simply ask, "What have you done with what you have been given?"

It could be argued that in our current ecological crisis in creation we are already experiencing the judgment of God. We are paying quite a cost for our sinful use and abuse of God's gifts. And yet even in our sin, God continues to be gracious. By God's grace, there is still time—time for us to change our ways, to repent and truthfully own up to the harm we have done, and to live more faithfully in the good creation we have been given. Karl Barth noted that God's judgment is yet another aspect of God's grace.

Thus for me these essays have been both judgment and grace. We shall be held to account—our sin shall exact a heavy price from us—but by God's grace, and the guidance of these Christian friends, there is still time. Thanks be to God!

Bibliography

Adams, James Eli. "Woman Red in Tooth and Claw: Nature and the Feminine in Tennyson and Darwin." *Victorian Studies* 33 (1989) 7–27.

Alexis-Baker, Nekeisha. "Doesn't the Bible Say that Humans Are More Important than Animals?" In *A Faith Embracing All Creatures: Addressing Commonly Asked Questions about Christian Care for Animals*, edited by Andy Alexis-Baker and Tripp York, 39–52. Eugene, OR: Cascade, 2012.

Ashenburg, Katherine. "Our Enemy Hands." *The New York Times,* November 27, 2007, A31.

Augustine. *Concerning the City of God against the Pagans*. Translated by Henry Bettenson. New York: Penguin, 1972.

Barth, Karl. *Church Dogmatics* III/1. *The Doctrine of Creation*. Edinburgh: T. & T. Clark, 1958.

Basil, Saint. "On the Hexaemeron." Translated by Agnes Clare Way. In *Exegetic Homilies*, 3–150. Washington, DC: Catholic University of America Press, 1963.

Bauckham, Richard. *The Bible and Ecology: Rediscovering the Community of Creation*. Waco, TX: Baylor University Press, 2010.

———. *Living with Other Creatures*. Waco, TX: Baylor University Press, 2011.

Benedict XVI, Pope. *Caritas in Veritate*. San Francisco: Ignatius, 2009.

———. "Fighting Poverty to Build Peace: World Day of Peace Message." January 1, 2009. http://www.vatican.va/holy_father/benedict_xvi/messages/peace/documents/hf_ben-xvi_mes_20081208_xlii-world-day-peace_en.html.

———. "The Human Family, a Community of Peace: World Day of Peace Message." January 1, 2008. http://www.vatican.va/holy_father/benedict_xvi/messages/peace/documents/hf_ben-xvi_mes_20071208_xli-world-day-peace_en.html.

Berry, Wendell. *Home Economics*. San Francisco: North Point, 1987.

———. *Sex, Economy, Freedom, and Community*. New York: Pantheon, 1993.

———. *What Are People For?* San Francisco: North Point, 1990.

Bittman, Mark. "Eating Meat Is Only Human." *The New York Times Diner's Journal*, February 5, 2008, 2012, http://dinersjournal.blogs.nytimes.com/2008/02/05/eating-meat-is-only-human/.

Bonaventure, Saint. "The Soul's Journey into God." Translated by Ewert Cousins. In *Bonaventure: The Soul's Journey into God, The Tree of Life, The Life of St. Francis*, 51–116. London: SPCK, 1978.

Bonhoeffer, Dietrich. *Creation and Fall: A Theological Interpretation of Genesis 1–3*. New York: Macmillan, 1959.

Bouma-Prediger, Steven. "Creation as the Home of God: The Doctrine of Creation in the Theology of Jurgen Moltmann." *Calvin Theological Journal* 31 (1997) 72–90.

———. *For the Beauty of the Earth.* 2nd ed. Grand Rapids: Baker Academic, 2010.

———. *The Greening of Theology.* Atlanta: Scholars, 1995.

Brown, William. *The Seven Pillars of Creation: The Bible, Science, and the Ecology of Wonder.* New York: Oxford University Press, 2010.

Brueggemann, Walter. *The Land: Place as Gift, Promise, and Challenge in Biblical Faith.* Philadelphia: Fortress, 1977.

Bynum, Carolyn Walker. *The Resurrection of the Body in Western Christianity, 200–1336.* New York: Columbia University Press, 1995.

Calvin, John. *Institutes of the Christian Religion.* Edited by John T. McNeill. Translated by Ford Lewis Battles. Philadelphia: Westminster, 1960.

Catechism of the Catholic Church. Vatican City: Libreria Editrice Vaticana, 1994.

Childs, Craig. "Rule of the Phoenix: On the Ephemeral Nature of Civilizations." *Orion* 31 (2012) 16–25.

Climate Central. *Global Weirdness: Severe Storms, Deadly Heat Waves, Relentless Drought, Rising Seas, and the Weather of the Future.* New York: Pantheon, 2012.

Cole, Leslie. "Conscious Carnivores, Ethical Butchers Are Changing Food Culture." *Oregon Live,* January 26, 2010, http://www.oregonlive.com/foodday/index.ssf/2010/01/the_conscious_carnivore.html.

Croke, Vicki. *The Modern Ark: The Story of Zoos: Past, Present and Future.* New York: Scribner, 1997.

Dailey, Anne. "The Conscious Carnivore." *Last Exit,* October 2, 2009, http://lastexitmag.com/article/the-conscious-carnivore.

Dante. *Paradise.* Translated by Mark Musa. New York: Penguin, 1986.

Davis, Ellen F. *Scripture, Culture, and Agriculture: An Agrarian Reading of the Bible.* New York: Cambridge University Press, 2009.

———. "Tikkun of the Fertile Soil." *Tikkun* 26 (2011) 36.

Deane-Drummond, Celia. *Christ and Evolution: Wonder and Wisdom.* Minneapolis: Fortress, 2009.

———. "Creation." In *Systematic Theology for a Changing Climate,* edited by Michael Northcott and Peter Scott. London: T. & T. Clark, in press.

———. *Creation through Wisdom: Theology and the New Biology.* Edinburgh: T. & T. Clark, 2000.

———. "Living from the Sabbath: Developing an Ecological Theology in the Context of Biodiversity." *Interface* 7 (2004) 1–13.

Diamond, Jared. *Collapse: How Societies Choose to Fail or Succeed.* New York: Viking, 2005.

Diels, H., and W. Kranz, eds. *Die Fragmente der Vorsokratiker.* 6th ed. 3 vols. Berlin: Weidmann, 1951–.

Dunn, James D. G. *The Theology of Paul the Apostle.* Grand Rapids: Eerdmans, 1998.

Ellul, Jacques. *On Freedom, Love, and Power.* Translated by William Vanderburg. Toronto: University of Toronto Press, 2010.

Environmental Investigation Agency. *The Illegal Logging Crisis in Honduras.* http://www.eia-international.org/wp-content/uploads/Honduras-Report-English-low-res.pdf.

Foer, Jonathan Safran. *Eating Animals.* New York: Little, Brown, 2009.

"Food as Spiritual and Political Praxis 2: Continuing the Conversation Between Autumn Brown and Nekeisha Alexis-Baker." http://www.jesusradicals.com/food-as-spiritual-and-political-praxis-2-continuing-the-conversation.

Fraser, Caroline. *Rewilding the World: Dispatches from the Conservation Revolution.* New York: Metropolitan, 2009.

French, Thomas. *Zoo Story: Life in the Garden of Captives.* New York: Hyperion, 2010.

Glendinning, Chellis. *When Technology Wounds: The Human Consequences of Progress.* New York: William Morrow, 1990.

Goodland, Robert, and Jeff Anhang. "Livestock and Climate Change." *World Watch*, November/December 2009, 10–19.

Gowan, Donald. *Eschatology in the Old Testament.* London: T. & T. Clark, 2000.

Gregerson, Niels. "Deep Incarnation: Why Evolutionary Continuity Matters in Christology." *Toronto Journal of Theology* 26 (2010) 173–87.

Hall, Lee. "Sustainable, Free-Range Farms and Other Tall Tales: Factory Farming's Not the Problem—It's Animal Farming." *Dissident Voice*, November 18, 2005, http://www.dissidentvoice.org/Nov05/Hall1118.htm.

Halteman, Matthew. "Varieties of Harm to Animals in Industrial Farming." *Journal of Animal Ethics* 1 (2011) 122–31.

Hargrove, Thomas, and Guido H. Stempel. "Most Americans Don't Believe in the Resurrection." *ReligionNewsBlog*, April 9, 2006, http://www.religionnewsblog.com/14273/most-americans-dont-believe-in-the-resurrection.

Heifetz, Ronald. *Leadership without Easy Answers.* Cambridge: Belknap Press of Harvard University Press, 1994.

Heifetz, Ronald, Alexander Grashow, and Marty Linsky. *The Practice of Adaptive Leadership: Tools and Tactics for Changing Your Organization and the World.* Boston: Harvard Business Press, 2009.

Hemenway, Toby. *Gaia's Garden: A Guide to Home-Scale Permaculture.* White River Junction, VT: Chelsea Green, 2009.

Hiebert, Theodore. *The Yahwist's Landscape: Nature and Religion in Early Israel.* New York: Oxford University Press, 1996.

Himes, Michael, and Kenneth Himes. "The Sacrament of Creation: Toward an Environmental Theology." *Commonweal*, January 26, 1990, 42–43.

Homer-Dixon, Thomas. *The Ingenuity Gap: How Can We Solve the Problems of the Future?* New York: Knopf, 2000.

Hultgren, Arland. "Eschatology in the New Testament: The Current Debate." In *The Last Things: Biblical and Theological Perspectives on Eschatology*, edited by Carl Braaten and Robert Jenson, 67–89. Grand Rapids: Eerdmans, 2002.

John Paul II, Pope. *Centesimus Annus.* 1991. http://www.vatican.va/holy_father/john_paul_ii/encyclicals/documents/hf_jp-ii_enc_01051991_centesimus-annus_en.html.

———. "Peace with God the Creator, Peace with All of Creation: World Day of Peace Message." January 1, 1990. In *The Green Bible*, I-35–I-42. San Francisco: HarperOne, 2008.

———. *Sollicitudo Rei Socialis.* December 30, 1987. http://www.vatican.va/holy_father/john_paul_ii/encyclicals/documents/hf_jp-ii_enc_30121987_sollicitudo-rei-socialis_en.html.

Johnson, Elizabeth. "An Earthly Christology." *America: The National Catholic Weekly*, April 13, 2009, 27–30.

Johnson, Kelly. *The Fear of Beggars: Poverty and Stewardship in Christian Ethics*. Grand Rapids: Eerdmans, 2007.

Jowit, Juliette. "UN Says Eat Less Meat to Curb Global Warming." *The Observer*, September 6, 2008, http://www.guardian.co.uk/environment/2008/sep/07/food.foodanddrink.

Kaminer, Ariel. "The Main Course Had an Unhappy Face . . ." *The New York Times*, November 19, 2012, http://www.nytimes.com/2010/11/21/nyregion/21citycritic.html.

Keller, Catherine. *Face of the Deep: A Theology of Becoming*. New York: Routledge, 2003.

King, Martin Luther, Jr. "Where Do We Go from Here: Chaos or Community?" In *A Testament of Hope: The Essential Writings and Speeches of Martin Luther King Jr.*, edited by James M. Washington, 555–633. San Francisco: HarperSanFrancisco, 1986.

Kittel, Gerhard, Gerhard Friedrich, and Geoffrey William Bromiley. *Theological Dictionary of the New Testament*. Grand Rapids: Eerdmans, 1985.

Kunstler, James Howard. "Ten Ways to Prepare for a Post-Oil Society." February 9, 2007. http://www.alternet.org/story/47705/ten_ways_to_prepare_for_a_post-oil_society.

————. *Too Much Magic: Wishful Thinking, Technology, and the Fate of the Nation*. New York: Atlantic Monthly, 2012.

Livestock's Long Shadow: Environmental Issues and Options. Rome: Food and Agriculture Organization of the United Nations, 2006.

Marrin, Albert. *War and the Christian Conscience: From Augustine to Martin Luther King, Jr.* Chicago: Regnery, 1971.

Maurin, Peter. *Easy Essays*. Chicago: Franciscan Herald, 1997.

McGinn, Bernard. "Do Christian Platonists Really Believe in Creation?" In *God and Creation*, edited by David Burrell and Bernard McGinn, 197–219. Notre Dame: University of Notre Dame Press, 1991.

McKibben, Bill. *The Comforting Whirlwind : God, Job, and the Scale of Creation*. Cambridge, MA: Cowley, 2005.

————. *The End of Nature*. New York: Random House, 1989.

Merton, Thomas. *Dancing in the Water of Life: The Journals of Thomas Merton*. Vol. 5, *1963–65*. San Francisco: HarperSanFrancisco, 1997.

————. *No Man Is an Island*. New York: Harcourt, Brace, 1955.

————. *Turning Toward the World: The Journals of Thomas Merton*. Edited by Victor Kramer San Francisco: HarperSanFrancisco, 1996.

Mitcham, Carl. "Technology as a Theological Problem in the Christian Tradition." In *Theology and Technology: Essays in Christian Analysis and Exegesis*, edited by Carl Mitcham and Jim Grote, 3–20. Lanham, MD: University Press of America, 1984.

Moltmann, Jürgen. *God in Creation*. San Francisco: Harper & Row, 1985.

Moo, Douglas. "Nature in the New Creation: New Testament Eschatology and the Environment." *Journal of the Evangelical Theological Society* 49 (2006) 449–88.

Morgan, Timothy. "The Mother of All Muddles." *Christianity Today*, April 5, 1993, 62–66.

Morris, Thomas. *Our Idea of God*. Downers Grove, IL: InterVarsity, 1991.

Myers, Ched. *The Biblical Vision of Sabbath Economics*. Washington, DC: Tell the Word, 2001.

―――. *Binding the Strong Man: A Political Reading of Mark's Story of Jesus*. Maryknoll, NY: Orbis, 2008.

―――. "The Cedar Has Fallen! The Prophetic Word versus Imperial Clear-Cutting." In *Earth and Word: Classic Sermons on Saving the Planet*, edited by David Rhoads, 211–22. New York: Continuum, 2007.

―――. "Everything Will Live Where the River Goes: A Bible Study on Water, God and Redemption." *Sojourners*, April 2012, 33–35.

―――. "A House for *All* Peoples? A Bible Study on Welcoming the Outsider." *Sojourners*, March 2006, 20–25.

Myers, Ched, and Eric Debode. "Towering Trees and 'Talented Slaves.'" *The Other Side*, May-June 1999, 10–15.

Nierenberg, Danielle. *Happier Meals: Rethinking the Global Meat Industry*. Danvers, MA: Worldwatch Institute, 2005.

Noble, David. *Progress Without People: New Technology, Unemployment, and the Message of Resistance*. Toronto: Between the Lines, 1995.

Norgaard, Kari Marie. *Living in Denial: Climate Change, Emotions, and Everyday Life*. Cambridge: MIT Press, 2011.

Northcott, Michael. *The Environment and Christian Ethics*. New York: Cambridge University Press, 1996.

O'Donovan, Oliver. *Resurrection and Moral Order: An Outline for Evangelical Ethics*. Grand Rapids: Eerdmans, 1994.

Oliver, Claudio. *Relationality: The Economic Conspiracy Project*. Philadelphia: Relational Tithe, 2010.

Parks, Sharon Daloz. *Leadership Can Be Taught*. Boston: Harvard Business School Press, 2005.

Patriarch Bartholomew of Constantinople. "Message for the Day of the Protection of the Environment." http://www.patriarchate.org/documents/2003-encyclical.

Paul VI, Pope. *Gaudium et Spes*. December 7, 1965. http://www.vatican.va/archive/hist_councils/ii_vatican_council/documents/vat-ii_cons_19651207_gaudium-et-spes_en.html.

―――. *Octogesima Adveniens*. May 14, 1971. http://www.vatican.va/holy_father/paul_vi/apost_letters/documents/hf_p-vi_apl_19710514_octogesima-adveniens_en.html.

―――. *Populorum Progressio*. March 26, 1967. http://www.vatican.va/holy_father/paul_vi/encyclicals/documents/hf_p-vi_enc_26031967_populorum_en.html.

Plutarch. "On the Eating of Flesh." In *Moralia*, translated by Frank Cole Babbitt, 540–79. Loeb Classical Library. Cambridge: Harvard University Press, 1957.

Pollan, Michael. *The Omnivore's Dilemma: A Natural History of Four Meals*. New York: Penguin, 2006.

Pontifical Council for Justice and Peace. "Compendium of the Social Doctrine of the Church." 2004. http://www.vatican.va/roman_curia/pontifical_councils/justpeace/documents/rc_pc_justpeace_doc_20060526_compendio-dott-soc_en.html.

Powlesland, Jim. "Eating Meat Is Natural." July 1996. http://people.ucalgary.ca/~powlesla/personal/hunting/rights/meat.txt.

Rolston, Holmes. "Feeding People Versus Saving Nature?" In *World Hunger and Morality*, edited by William Aiken and Hugh LaFollette, 248–67. Englewood Cliffs, NJ: Prentice-Hall, 1996.

Rossing, Barbara. "River of Life in God's New Jerusalem: An Eschatological Vision for Earth's Future." In *Christianity and Ecology*, edited by Dieter Hessel and Rosemary Radford Ruether, 205–24. Cambridge: Center for the Study of World Religions, 2000.

Russell, David. *The "New Heavens and New Earth": Hope for the Creation in Jewish Apocalyptic and the New Testament*. Philadelphia: Visionary, 1996.

Russell, Jeffrey Burton. *A History of Heaven: The Singing Silence*. Princeton: Princeton University Press, 1997.

Sachs, Wolfgang. "Environment." In *The Development Dictionary: A Guide to Knowledge as Power*, edited by Wolfgang Sachs, 26–37. 2nd ed. London: Zed, 2010.

Santmire, H. Paul. *Nature Reborn*. Minneapolis: Augsburg Fortress, 2000.

————. *Ritualizing Nature*. Minneapolis: Fortress, 2008.

————. *The Travail of Nature*. Philadelphia: Fortress, 1985.

Sarna, Nahum. *Genesis*. JPS Torah Commentary. Philadelphia: Jewish Publication Society, 1989.

Schifferdecker, Kathryn. *Out of the Whirlwind: Creation Theology in the Book of Job*. Cambridge: Harvard University Press, 2008.

Scully, Matthew. *Dominion: The Power of Man, the Suffering of Animals, and the Call to Mercy*. 1st ed. New York: St. Martin's, 2002.

Sellers, Patricia. "Mark Zuckerberg's New Challenge: Eating Only What He Kills (and Yes, We Do Mean Literally . . .)" *Fortune*, May 26, 2011, http://postcards.blogs.fortune.cnn.com/2011/05/26/mark-zuckerbergs-new-challenge-eating-only-what-he-kills/.

Sheen, Fulton J. The Life of All Living. New York: Popular Library, 1929.

Shiva, Vandava. "Resources." In *The Development Dictionary: A Guide to Knowledge as Power*, edited by Wolfgang Sachs, 206–18. 2nd ed. London: Zed, 2010.

Sittler, Joseph. "Ecological Commitment as Theological Responsibility." *Zygon* 5 (1970) 172–81.

————. *Gravity and Grace*. Minneapolis: Augsburg, 1986.

————. *The Structure of Christian Ethics*. Baton Rouge: Louisiana State University Press, 1958.

Steingraber, Sandra. *Living Downstream: An Ecologist Looks at Cancer and the Environment*. New York: Addison-Wesley, 1997.

Stonich, Susan, and Billie DeWalt. "The Political Ecology of Deforestation in Honduras." In *The Environment in Anthropology: A Reader in Ecology, Culture, and Sustainable Living*, edited by Nora Haenn and Richard Wilk, 284–301. New York: New York University Press, 2006.

Strong, David. *Crazy Mountains: Learning from Wilderness to Weigh Technology*. Albany: State University of New York Press, 1995.

Taylor, Barbara Brown. *When God Is Silent*. Cambridge, MA: Cowley, 1998.

Telford, William. *The Barren Temple and the Withered Tree*. JSNT Supplementary Series 1. Sheffield: JSOT, 1980.

Tenner, Edward. *Why Things Bite Back: Technology and the Revenge of Unintended Consequences*. New York: Knopf, 1996.

Theological Dictionary of the New Testament. Edited by Gerhard Kittel and Gerhard Friedrich; translated by Geoffrey W. Bromiley; abridged in one volume by Geoffrey W. Bromiley. Grand Rapids: Eerdmans, 1985.

Thomas, Aquinas, Saint. *Summa Theologiae*. Translated by English Dominicans. London: Oates & Washbourne, 1952.

Thoreau, Henry David. *Walden, Or, Life in the Woods*. 2 vols. Boston: Houghton Mifflin, 1897.

Tinker, George. "Spirituality, Native American Personhood, Sovereignty and Solidarity." *The Ecumenical Review* 44 (1992) 312–24.

Vandenack, Tim. "Offal Will Help Fuel Middlebury Duck Farm." *The Elkhart Truth*, August 17, 2012, A3.

Vann, Gerald. *The Water and the Fire*. New York: Sheed and Ward, 1954.

Weisman, Alan. *The World Without Us*. New York: St. Martin's, 2007.

Westermann, Claus. *Genesis 1–11*. Translated by John Scullion. Minneapolis: Augsburg, 1984.

White, Lynn. "The Historical Roots of Our Ecologic Crisis." *Science*, March 10, 1967, 1203–7.

White, Mel. "Path of the Jaguar." *National Geographic*, March 2009, 123–33.

Wirzba, Norman. "Barnyard Dance: Farming that Honors Animals." *Christian Century*, January 23, 2007, 8–9.

Wolterstorff, Nicholas. "God Everlasting." In *God and the Good*, edited by Clifton Orlebeke and Lewis Smedes, 181–203. Grand Rapids: Eerdmans, 1975.

Worldwatch Institute. *State of the World 2004*. New York: Routledge, 2004.

Wright, N. T. *The Resurrection of the Son of God*. Minneapolis: Fortress, 2003.

———. *Surprised by Hope* London: SPCK, 2007.